Crowding out the Future

World Population Growth,
U.S. Immigration, and
Pressures on Natural Resources

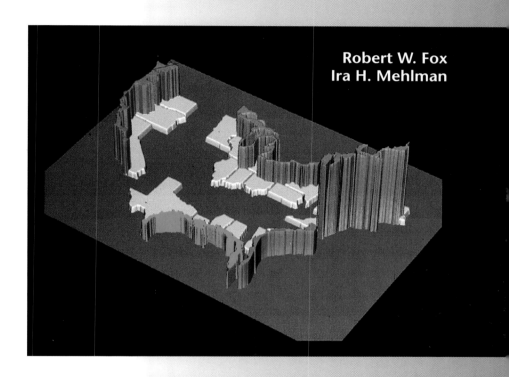

Robert W. Fox
Ira H. Mehlman

Federation for American Immigration Reform
1666 Connecticut Avenue, NW
Washington, DC 20009

Foreword

This publication seeks to illustrate through text, graphics, satellite imagery and data three main points. 1) Rapid world population growth is placing untenable immigration pressures on the United States. 2) Immigration and U.S. population growth patterns generally are regionally-concentrated, especially in coastal counties. This coastal county growth has far-reaching consequences that affect other parts of the nation and even the rest of the world. 3) Given population and natural resource/environmental pressures, there are now profound and urgent reasons to address immigration within a broader national population policy framework. Left unchecked, immigration will soon be America's most important population issue.

Rapid population growth in the world's less developed regions, combined with the development of modern communications and transportation technology, is creating and facilitating unprecedented international migration pressures.

The United Nations estimates that 90 million people are now added to the population of the planet each year. Within the next decade, more people will be added than there were in the entire world in 1800. Just two generations ago, global population was 2.5 billion. During 1992, we will reach the 5.5 billion mark, and the UN estimates that we will exceed 10 billion in the next century before population growth levels off.

This powerful demographic force will explode in an unprecedented wave of human migration in the 21st century as tens of millions seek economic opportunity and escape from environmental disaster. The patterns have just begun to emerge and will grow with intensity in the decades to come.

In much of the less developed world we have witnessed the flight from rural to urban areas over the past two generations. Those in the countryside are moving—voting with their feet—in response to poor and declining living conditions. Pushed from the countryside and pulled by the city's bright lights and economic opportunity—real or imagined—tens of millions have elected to crowd into teeming metropolitan areas. Mexico City, for example, with 3.5 million people as recently as 1950, now holds around 18 million. And what we have witnessed to date is only the tip of the iceberg. The UN estimates that between 1987 and 2025, the urban population of the Third World will have grown by 2.75 billion people—twice the amount that were added during the period from 1950 to 1987.

Along with rapid urbanization, the population explosion in the less developed world has resulted in a vast labor force increase. The huge cohort born in the 1970s is only now entering the labor market, overwhelming the economies of many poorer nations. The Third World labor force has increased by more than 500 million since 1975. By 2025, another 1.4 billion people will be seeking employment, a number more than double the present total labor force of the more developed regions.

The great majority of these workers will be urban based or urban bound. In country after country, however, urban unemployment and underemployment already run high, affecting as much as half the labor force. Still, there are millions of new entrants each year, the products of rapid population growth from a generation earlier. Driven by rising expectations but facing plummeting prospects, great numbers have determined to take their chances and migrate, legally or illegally, to destinations in the more developed countries.

World population increase, urbanization and labor force growth are all topics covered in this publication. To grasp the dynamics that fuel the population explosion, a detailed look is taken at each of the key components in the demographic mix. They include the startling differences in age distribution patterns between the more and less developed regions of the world, the vast rise in the number of women of reproductive age and their fertility levels and, finally, the number of births by world region.

The second portion of the publication focuses on the United States, its population growth and linkages to select natural resources (including energy consumption) and environmental issues. The United States has the fastest growing population of any industrialized nation and that growth has a significant effect on the global environment and the quality of life in the U.S. Today, more than half the United States' population growth is attributable to immigrants and their offspring. At a time of growing migration pressures around the world, we must also face the reality that resource consumption and environmental considerations limit the number of people the United States can absorb.

The United States cannot be a destination of large scale immigration forever. When the Statue of Liberty was erected in New York harbor, this was a nation of 60 million people with a largely unsettled west and an economy embarking on the industrial revolution. Today we are a nation of a quarter of a billion people facing the problems of urban congestion, resource shortages and a rapidly changing economy that requires highly specialized skills, not merely strong backs. Evidence suggests that we are already an overcrowded nation. Nevertheless, the United States continues to admit more immigrants than all other nations on earth combined, and more than at any time in our history. Population in the United States has grown to the point where it now threatens to do irreparable harm to our environment.

We hope the materials in this report will demonstrate the national urgency of restraining U.S. population growth through responsible limits on immigration and immigration reform as well as effective family planning programs.

Dan Stein, Executive Director

World Regions (countries listed are those with more than 300,000 population in 1990)

Eastern Africa:
Burundi, Comoros, Djibouti, Ethiopia, Kenya, Madagascar, Malawi, Mauritius, Mozambique, Reunion, Rwanda, Somalia, Uganda, Tanzania, Zambia, Zimbabwe.

Middle Africa:
Angola, Cameroon, Central African Republic, Chad, Congo, Equatorial Guinea, Gabon, Zaire.

Northern Africa:
Algeria, Egypt, Libya, Morocco, Sudan, Tunisia.

Southern Africa:
Botswana, Lesotho, Namibia, South Africa, Swaziland.

Western Africa:
Benin, Burkina Faso, Cape Verde, Cote d'Ivoire, Gambia, Ghana, Guinea, Guinea-Bissau, Liberia, Mali, Mauritania, Niger, Nigeria, Senegal, Sierra Leone, Togo.

Caribbean:
Cuba, Dominican Republic, Guadeloupe, Haiti, Jamaica, Martinique, Puerto Rico, Trinidad and Tobago.

Central America:
Costa Rica, El Salvador, Guatemala, Honduras, Mexico, Nicaragua, Panama.

Temperate South America:
Argentina, Chile, Uruguay.

Tropical South America:
Bolivia, Brazil, Colombia, Ecuador, Guyana, Paraguay, Peru, Suriname, Venezuela.

Northern America:
Canada, United States.

China

Japan

Other East Asia:
Hong Kong, People's Republic of Korea, Republic of Korea, Macau, Mongolia.

Southeastern Asia:
Cambodia, East Timor, Indonesia, Laos, Malaysia, Myanmar, Philippines, Singapore, Thailand, Vietnam.

Southern Asia:
Afghanistan, Bangladesh, Bhutan, Iran, Nepal, Pakistan, Sri Lanka.

India

Western Asia:
Bahrain, Cyprus, Gaza Strip, Iraq, Israel, Jordan, Kuwait, Lebanon, Oman, Qatar, Saudi Arabia, Syria, Turkey, United Arab Emirates, Yemen.

Eastern Europe:
Bulgaria, Czechoslovakia, Hungary, Poland, Romania.

Northern Europe:
Denmark, Finland, Ireland, Norway, Sweden, United Kingdom.

Southern Europe:
Albania, Greece, Italy, Malta, Portugal, Spain, (former) Yugoslavia.

Western Europe:
Austria, Belgium, France, Germany, Luxembourg, Netherlands, Switzerland.

Oceania:
Australia, Fiji, New Zealand, Papua New Guinea, Solomon Islands.

U.S.S.R.:
All republics comprising the former U.S.S.R.

Table of Contents

The Ethics of Population Growth and Immigration Control
by Garrett Hardin

To speak of a "world population problem" is to imply there is a worldwide solution. But how can there be? Nearly two hundred nations claim sovereignty, i.e., the right to solve their own problems. The 20th century began with idealistic dreams of "One World." The century is ending with a clear trend toward the fission of existing nations into more sovereign units. A realistic approach to population problems assumes a continuation of this trend.

Each sovereign nation must be held responsible for keeping its own population size under control. Outsiders can, however, influence a nation's population growth by sharing the technology of birth control. That is already being done. Unfortunately, experience has shown that mere knowledge of birth control is not enough to achieve a stable population. People must be convinced that the future will be better with population control than without it.

Under earlier, more primitive conditions no explicit policy was needed to control population. Nature took care of the matter. With variable food harvests and poor transportation, area-limited famines often reduced the population. Contagious diseases were capable of wiping out as much as 25 percent of a country's population in a single year.

Advances in agriculture, transportation, medicine and sanitation have changed all that. Populations are now growing at unprecedented rates. Human policy must take on a corrective function once performed by Nature. In some countries, moral or religious directives interfere with the control of reproduction. In such cases, ancient ethical principles will have to be modified if ruinous overpopulation is to be forestalled.

What about the United States? By virtue of mutual assimilation of divergent religious beliefs in the past, remaining differences seem, at this moment, not to be a major cause of continued population growth. Accelerating immigration is the major cause of population growth. Powerful forces support the continuance of immigration.

Some businessmen see immigration as a way to keep labor costs down. Employers seldom inquire into the suffering of employees who are displaced by newcomers. (If business executives could be easily replaced by immigrant executives, would immigration be so enthusiastically encouraged?). Any short-term gains must be balanced against the long-term disadvantages of reducing the per capita share of national resources.

The other encouragement to immigration is found in the source-countries themselves. By encouraging dissatisfied citizens to leave, a ruler can strengthen his political position. Cuba's Fidel Castro took this option in 1980 when 130,000 men, women and children were shipped off to Florida. A full year's increase in the island's population was disposed of—at American expense.

Yet there are those among us who think that we are morally required to share our national wealth with all the world because we are "our brother's keeper." Even granting the validity of the imperative, is it likely that removing some of a poor nation's excess population will solve its own population problem? Will those who are left behind be more or less fertile after the pressure of overpopulation is reduced?

Careful scientific studies of other species of animals show that the lowering of population pressure produces an increase in fertility. Human beings cannot be made the subject of carefully controlled experiments, so knowledge is less certain. But the bulk of the evidence indicates that human beings, like other organisms, respond rationally to changes in population. When times get really tough, people have fewer children. When population pressures diminish, human fertility rises. These responses make sense. We can confidently predict that removing the excess fertility from a poor and overpopulated country will produce a rise in fertility. Accepting the "superfluous" emigrants is no way to help a poor country solve its population problem!

And what about us, the receiving nation? Will more millions of immigrants put an end to our traffic jams? Increase the speed and safety of commuting? Do away with the overcrowding of national parks and other recreation areas? Decrease the size of our ghettos? Decrease the crime that comes with crowding?

As immigration increases will divergent cultures assimilate more rapidly to American standards? Will demands for multiple official languages cease? Will ever more diversity make political unity easier to achieve?

The answers are surely obvious. Though some individuals (employers, for example) may gain personally from immigration, the nation as a whole will lose. Our present population of a quarter of a billion is more than enough to exploit the resources with which we have been blessed. Too much exploitation can ruin an area: look at the eastern shores of the Mediterranean.

A traditional moralist may object, asserting: "I am my brother's keeper." We must ask him: "And what about your children? And your children's children? What about the children of your neighbor next door? Must we subdivide and distribute our patrimony among the children of all the world?" Americans are already outnumbered twenty-to-one by the rest of the world. Our grandchildren will be outnumbered even more. Must we condemn them to the poverty of an absolutely equal distribution? How would that benefit them or the descendants of other people?

Total poverty can be avoided only if people agree that the ancient admonition "Charity begins at home" is still the best guide to philanthropic action. The images that follow indicate that population control must also begin at home—at as many homes as there are sovereign nations in the world. The brothers and sisters in all sovereign states must accept the responsibility of solving their population problems in their own territories. ❑

7

The Population Explosion

The global population explosion began in earnest in the post-World War II era as significant gains were made in controlling diseases that had ravaged human populations throughout history. Advances in technology, nutrition, sanitation and health resulted in more people surviving childhood and living longer than ever before.

In the more developed world, these changes had occurred slowly, over a period of 150 years. In the less developed regions they occurred almost overnight. By 1970, the population growth rate in the developed countries had slowed to less than one percent annually and absolute increases would level off within a half century. In the less developed nations, populations continue to soar, in some cases doubling in the span of only 25 years.

The geometry of population growth means that even as the rate of population growth slows down, the actual number of people being added to the human population will remain high for decades to come—currently around 90 million a year. The doubling of our current population of 5.5 billion will be of far greater significance in terms of energy, resource consumption and stress on the environment than any previous doubling of worldwide population.

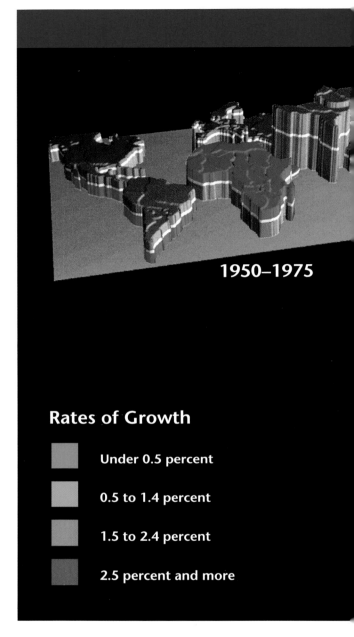

1950–1975

Rates of Growth

Under 0.5 percent

0.5 to 1.4 percent

1.5 to 2.4 percent

2.5 percent and more

Africa, shown in bright pink for the 1975-2000 period, stands out due to its very high population growth rate. Rates below 0.5 percent (in blue) can be characterized as moderate to low, 0.5-1.4 percent rates (in green) as moderate to moderately high, and rates above 1.5 percent (in orange and bright pink) as high to extremely high.

Vertical (or height) represents the total population size. The segment below the white line represents population size and the colors, the rate of population growth, at the beginning of the time period for each region. The segment above the line represents the net increase during that 25-year period and the colors, the rate of growth at the end of the time period.

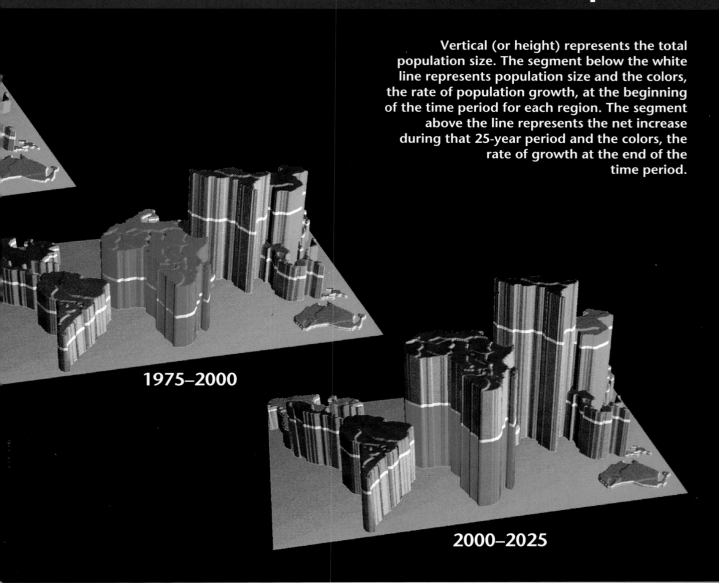

1975–2000

2000–2025

The population of Africa in 1950 was 224 million. By 1990, it increased to 640 million and is projected to be 1.6 billion by 2025.

The Surging Population of the Underdeveloped World

The global population explosion that has occurred since 1950 has not been evenly distributed. While the developed nations approach population stability (as China is doing), explosive increases will continue in most of the less developed countries.

This uneven growth has resulted in unevenly distributed pressures on the economic and social systems and on the environment. These are stressful situations further exacerbated by the rush toward urbanization. Just the incremental 25-year increases in the underdeveloped world far exceed the total population of the developed countries.

Countries with economic and social structures least capable of coping with rapid population growth have seen a half-century of explosive increases. Moreover, the greatest period of population growth in these countries still lies ahead.

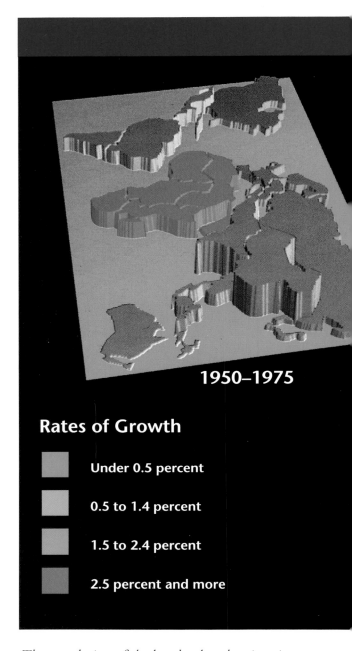

1950–1975

Rates of Growth

Under 0.5 percent

0.5 to 1.4 percent

1.5 to 2.4 percent

2.5 percent and more

The population of the less developed regions is projected to increase by 5.5 billion inhabitants between 1950 and 2025. Approximately 20 percent of that increase occurred between 1950 and 1975. The remainder, in nearly equal 40 percent shares, is anticipated for the periods between 1975-2000, and 2000-2025.

Net Population Increases

Vertical represents only the population increase in each 25-year time period. Colors depict the rate of growth for the last five-year period of each interval.

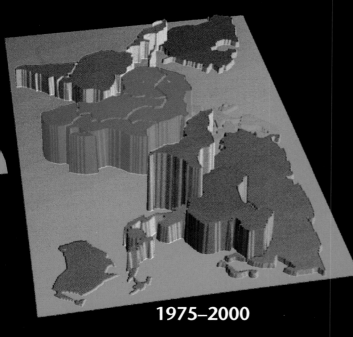

1975–2000

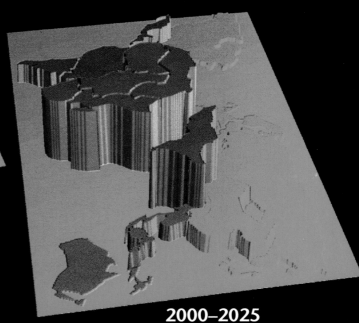

2000–2025

During 1950–1975, 83 percent of all population growth occurred in the less developed regions. During 2000–2025, 96 percent of world population growth is projected to occur in those areas.

The Transformation to an Urban World

Population growth and distribution trends in the less developed regions are increasingly characterized by urbanization. Societies that have been primarily agrarian throughout history have been transformed, in just a few years, into urban societies as a result. Most population increases in the less developed regions are now accruing to urban areas either through rural to urban migration or by natural increase (the excess of births over deaths) of the existing city population.

The movement of large numbers of people from rural to urban areas has created enormous pressures on the fledgling industrial economies in which many of these people seek economic opportunities. The rapid transformation of societies from rural to urban has also generated substantial social instability as people are displaced from their traditional cultures and support systems. Throughout the underdeveloped world, urban crowding and poverty are breeding grounds for civil unrest, violence and revolution. Much of the underdeveloped world's political instability is attributable to this phenomenon and, with the collapse of the Soviet empire, population growth and rapid urbanization are likely to be the greatest threats to world peace and a major source of migration pressure on wealthier and more stable nations like the United States.

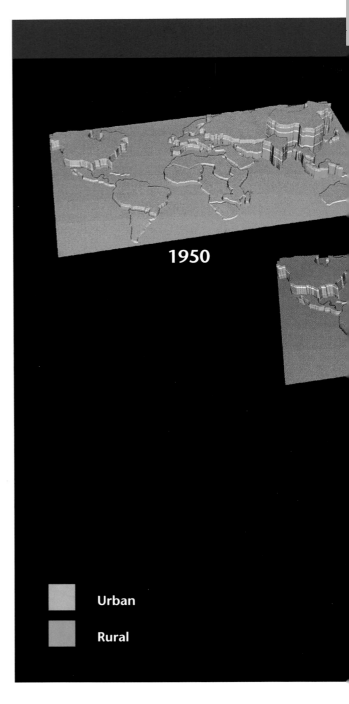

1950

Urban

Rural

In 1950, North America had an urban population of 108 million; Asia (excluding Japan) had an urban population of 175 million. In 1990, the figures were 207 million and 900 million, respectively. By 2025, North America is projected to have 280 million urban

Vertical represents total population. Urban population is shown in brown, rural in green. White bands represent increments of 200 million.

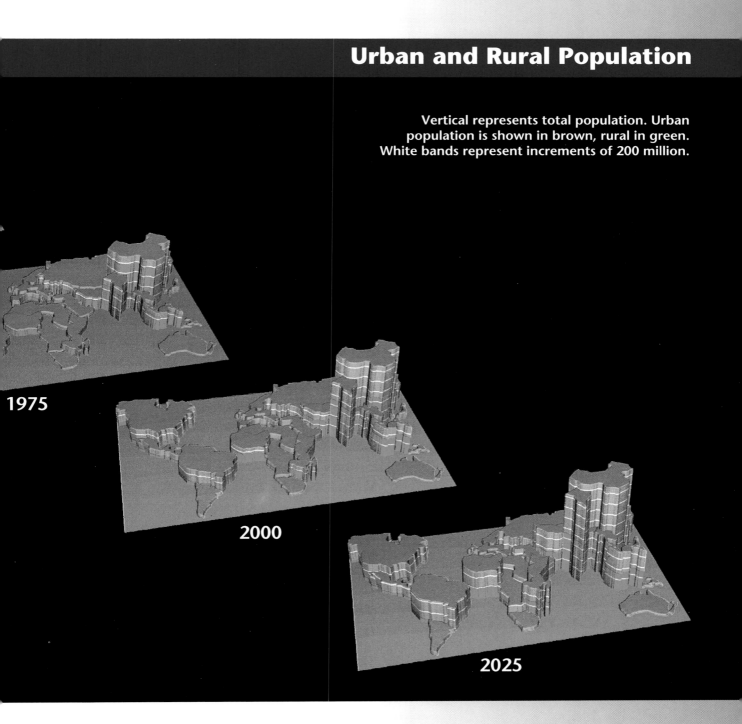

1975

2000

2025

dwellers, while Asia will have an urban population of 2.5 billion—roughly the population of the entire world in 1950.

Dividing Birth Shares Among World Regions

Population growth occurs when the number of births exceeds the number of deaths (absent migration). Throughout most of history, high birth rates were offset by high death rates. Thus, until the mid-19th century, human population grew very slowly. Beginning a century-and-a-half ago, many of the diseases that had limited human life spans began to be conquered in the now developed world. In the mid-20th century, these medical advances were extended to the underdeveloped world as well.

From about 1950 on, the age-old relationship between high birth and high death rates changed rapidly. Birth rates stayed high, while death rates dropped precipitously. The population explosion was underway as the gap between the two widened.

The birth rate began to decline moderately and then slightly faster in the 1970s and 1980s. Still, the actual number of births remained high as a result of "demographic momentum," ensuring that population will continue to increase even while birth rates fall.

Less developed regions continue to claim a high share of births worldwide. Eastern Africa stands as a perfect example. Its birth rate is falling, but given momentum factors—particularly the exceptionally large increase in women of reproductive age—the actual annual number of births will rise fivefold.

By contrast, the developed countries, which are nearing population stabilization, do not have the same kind of demographic momentum. Consequently, the developed world has both low birth rates and low numbers of births.

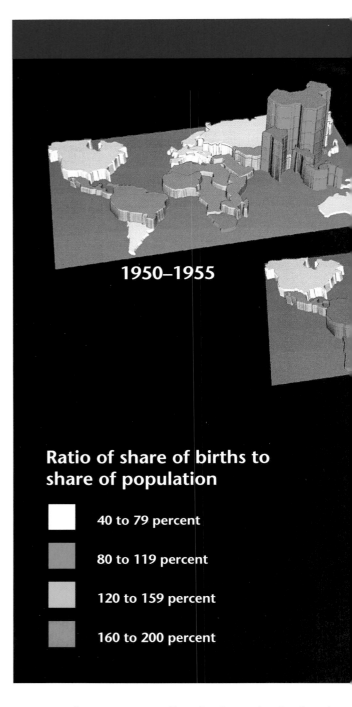

1950–1955

Ratio of share of births to share of population

- 40 to 79 percent
- 80 to 119 percent
- 120 to 159 percent
- 160 to 200 percent

In 1950 there were 19 million births in the developed countries. By 1990, that figure had declined to 16 million annually, a level where it is projected to remain through 2025. In the less developed regions there were 79 million births in 1950 and 125 million

Vertical represents the yearly number of births during the five-year intervals. Purple bands denote increments of 5 million. Colors represent pro rata share of world births to total population. If, for example, a region has 10 percent of the world's births and 10 percent of the world's population, its pro rata share is 100 percent. Alternatively, with 5 percent of the world's births but 10 percent of the world's population, its pro rata share is 50 percent.

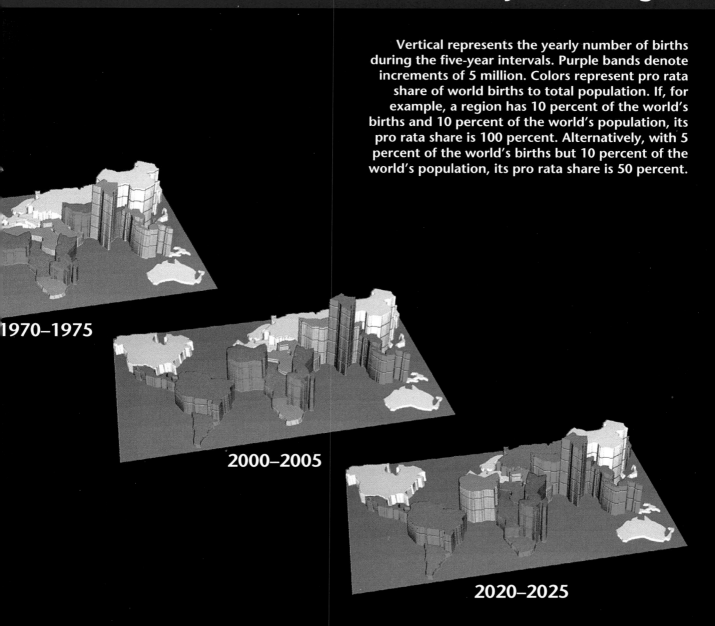

1970–1975

2000–2005

2020–2025

in 1990. That figure should rise slightly to 130 million a year before the end of the century and remain at that level through 2025.

Growth Momentum: The Increase in Women Ages 15 to 49

I n population growth terms, the critical group is the number of women of childbearing age. *Women of reproductive age are increasing ten times faster in the less developed regions than in the more developed countries.* This is the product of a cycle that emerged in the mid-20th century, combining high fertility with sharp increases in infant survival. The result is greater numbers of surviving children who themselves shortly become parents.

A paradox is presented of falling fertility alongside rising numbers of births and growing populations. Even though women in the less developed regions are now averaging fewer babies, there are now far more women. Thus, the number of total births continues to increase even with falling fertility.

Two of the factors necessary to approach population stabilization are that fertility continues to decline and the number of women having babies evolves to a peak and begins to diminish. The first condition is being met, as shown by the color shift in the graphics. However, the number of women 15–49 in the less developed regions is projected to continue to increase substantially.

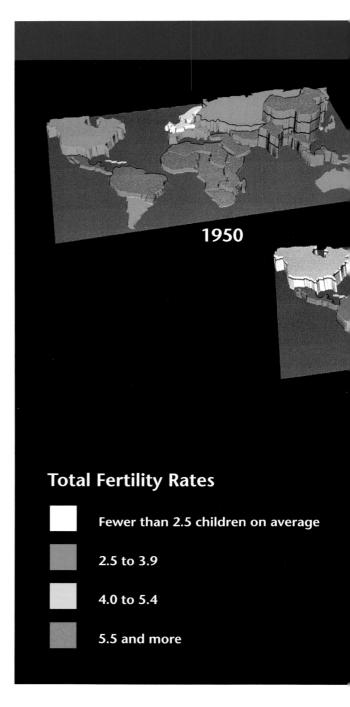

1950

Total Fertility Rates

Fewer than 2.5 children on average

2.5 to 3.9

4.0 to 5.4

5.5 and more

In 1950, there were 52 million women between the ages of 15–49 in Africa. By 1990, that number had grown to 155 million. By 2025 it is projected that there will be 418 million women of reproductive age in Africa—an eight-fold increase over 1950.

16

Vertical represents total number of women 15-49. Dark bands denote increments of 50 million. Colors correspond to total fertility rates, or the number of children born, on average, to each woman during her reproductive years.

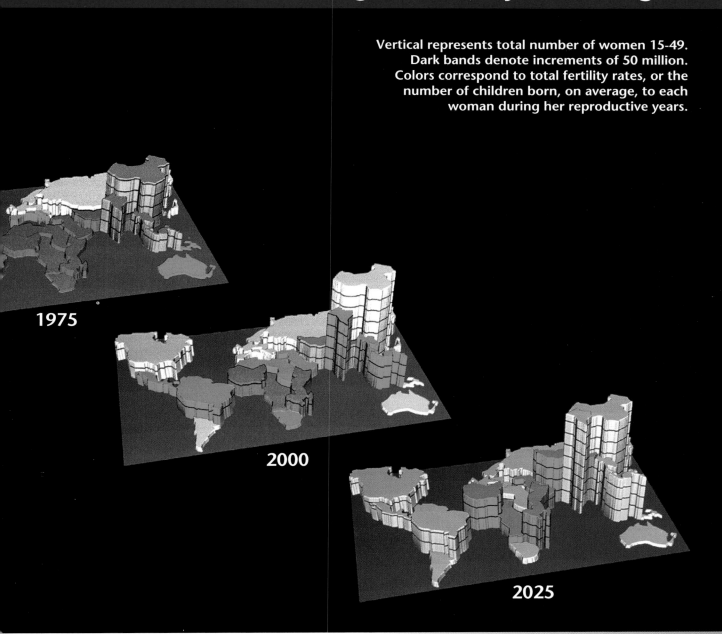

1975

2000

2025

In contrast, women ages 15–49 in the more developed regions will increase by less than one-third during that 75-year interval. There were 224 million such women in 1950, and 290 million are projected for 2025.

17

Two Distinct Age Distribution Patterns

The pyramid of the more developed regions reflects a relatively slow pace of population growth. As a region stabilizes its population, the traditional "population pyramid" is transformed, over time, into a more rectangular shape, as the size of all age groups within those societies becomes roughly equal. Despite frequently expressed concerns about an aging population in the more developed world, *a degree of "aging" is an inevitable consequence when societies begin to stabilize population size.*

Fast growth regions, on the other hand, continue to produce population pyramids with an ever-expanding base. A pause in the trend emerges in 1975–80 in the pyramid depicting the less developed regions, with a scallop effect spiraling upward in subsequent years that reflects the aging of this particular birth cohort. This is due largely to reduced births in China, which accounts for one-third of the less developed regions' population.

In much of the less developed world, half the population is under the age of 15. Even if the birth rates of these children are substantially lower than that of their parents, the sheer number of young people about to enter their reproductive years will continue to generate high numbers of births for many years to come.

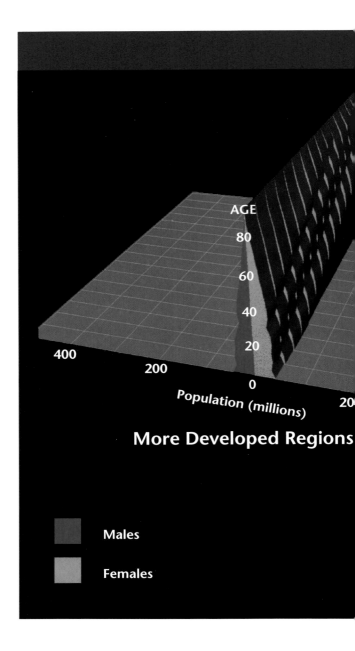

More Developed Regions

Males

Females

In 1990, 47 percent of the population of Western Africa was under the age of 15. In Western Europe and Japan, only 18 percent of the population was below 15.

18

The pyramid's vertical portion represents the age of the population in five-year increments. The horizontal axis represents the size of the population by sex. Depth represents change of the age structure over time.

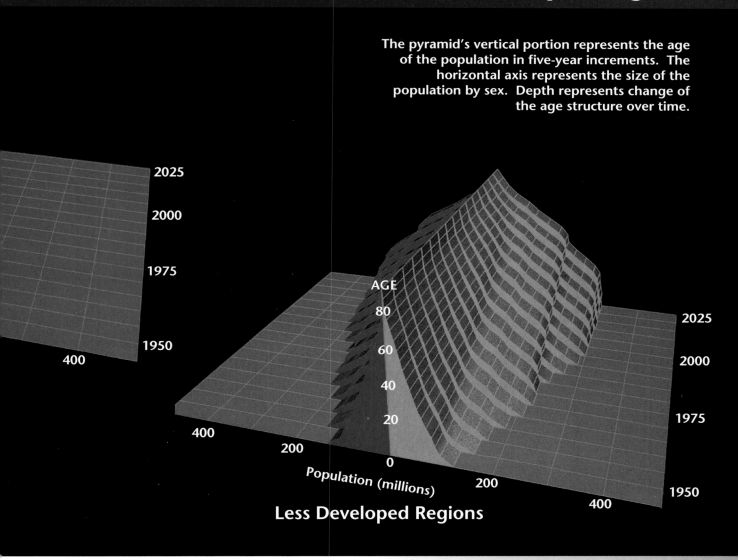

Less Developed Regions

Births Minus Deaths: The Mathematics of Population Growth

O ne of the great achievements of modern times is that more people are surviving early childhood and living longer lives than ever before. Though vast discrepancies still exist between the prosperous, developed countries and the impoverished underdeveloped countries, child mortality rates are falling and life expectancy is on the increase in all parts of the world.

In both the developed and underdeveloped areas the number of deaths is rising slowly. In the low population growth and more developed regions this is associated with the natural "aging" of the population. Here, 12 percent in 1990 were age 65 and older, compared to 4 percent in this age group in the less developed regions.

In the less developed countries, births have outpaced deaths about 2.5 to 1. Since 1950, there has been a sharp increase in the number of births in these countries. The absolute number of births is projected to level off at about 130 million annually by 1995.

The drop off in births between 1975 and 1980 (on the "less developed regions" graph) largely reflects China's efforts to reduce population growth and is an indication of the effect of vigorous family planning efforts.

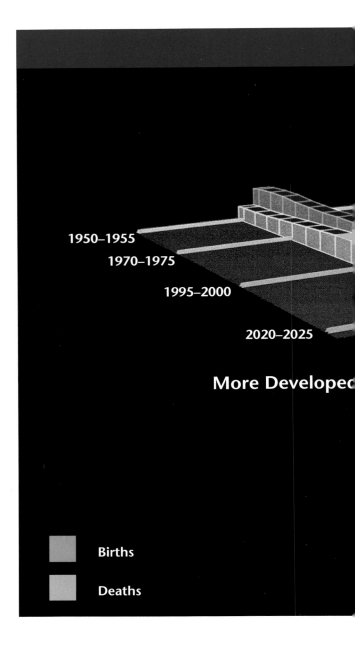

Between 1950 and 1955, the annual number of births in the less developed regions exceeded deaths by 36 million. By 2020–2025, the gap is projected to widen to 80 million. In the more developed regions, there were 11 million more births than deaths in 1950-1955. By 2020–2025, the number of births in these regions is expected to exceed deaths by only 2 million a year.

Vertical depicts the number of births and deaths (in millions). The excess of births over deaths represents population increase.

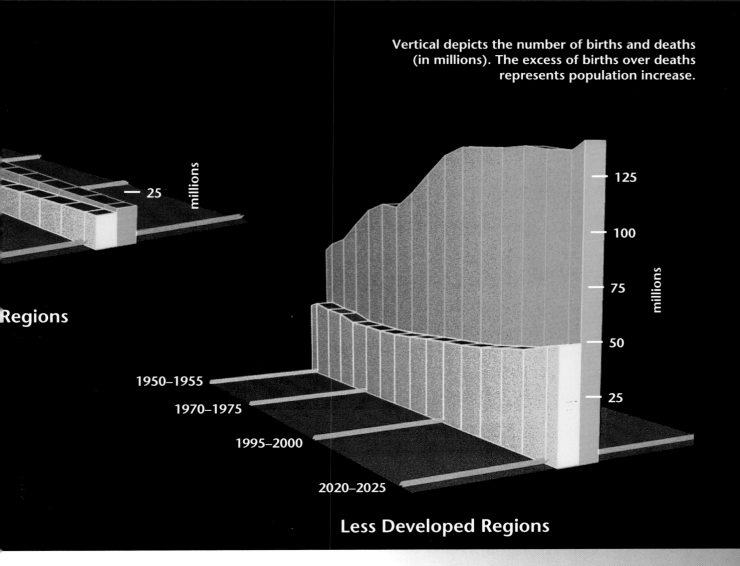

millions

25

Regions

1950–1955

1970–1975

1995–2000

2020–2025

125

100

75

50

25

millions

Less Developed Regions

21

Where Will the Jobs Come From?

One consequence of the explosive population increase in the less developed world is the growth of the labor force. Given the 15 to 20 year time lag between birth and entry into the labor force, we are only now beginning to see the effects of the high birth rates of the 1970s.

Throughout history people have migrated in search of economic opportunity. As unprecedented numbers of first time entrants join the labor forces of countries whose economies cannot now adequately provide for existing workers, many will look to the developed world to find rewarding economic activity. The migration of even a small percentage of these workers to the developed countries places enormous economic and social pressures on the countries to which they migrate. As the less developed world becomes increasingly urbanized, migrating urban workers will compete directly with workers in the urban centers of the developed regions.

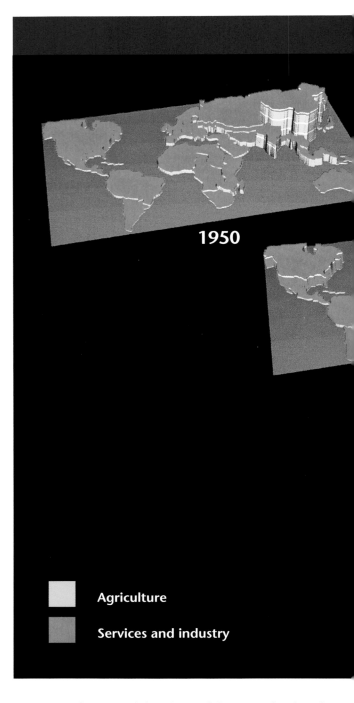

1950

■ Agriculture

■ Services and industry

In 1990, the entire labor force of the more developed regions was 584 million people. In just the next 10 years, the less developed countries will have to produce 372 million jobs to accommodate all the new labor

22

Yellow is agricultural labor force. Red is service and industry-based labor force. Vertical represents total labor force. White bands represent increments of 100 million workers.

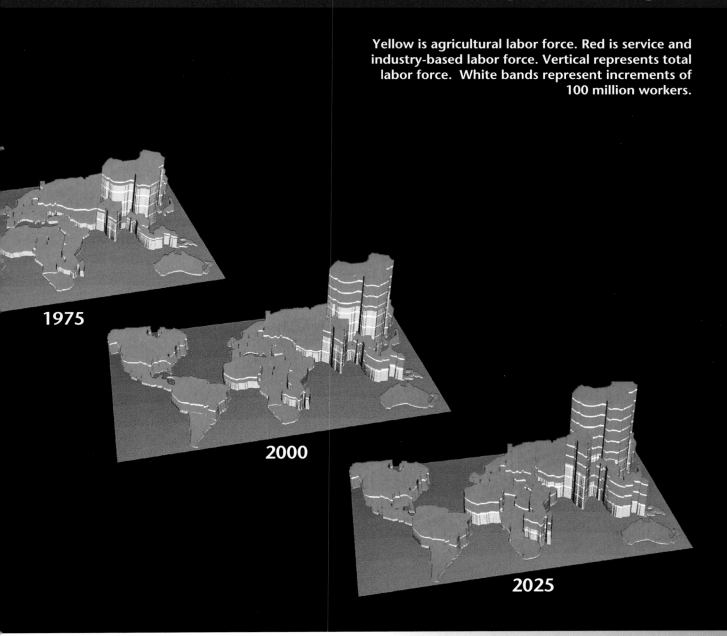

1975

2000

2025

force entrants. These are not projections. The workers of the early 21st century are already born.

The Ethics of U.S. Immigration Policy in an Overpopulated World
by Richard D. Lamm

Gunnar Myrdal, the noted Swedish sociologist, developed a concept he called the "braking distance" of population growth. He stated that stabilizing population is like stopping a car—one has to anticipate generations in advance. Even after a previously rapid-growth country reaches a replacement rate of 2.1 births per woman on average, the population will continue to grow for two or three generations. This concept shows the necessity to be far-sighted: Public policy must stop being reactionary and must begin to be anticipatory if we are to leave any kind of quality of life for our children.

Virtually everybody takes it as a given that at some point population growth must stop. No trees grow to the sky and a finite earth cannot absorb infinite people. If the United States should grow for the next 200 years at the same rate we grew during the last 200 years, there would be three times as many people in the United States than in the entire world today. Such a scenario is not only a nightmare, it is likely impossible. America, at some point, must stabilize its population. This demands that we realistically anticipate and ask ourselves how many people can live satisfying lives in the United States.

Without immigration, the United States would be on the road to population stabilization by the middle of the next century. This has happened by the voluntary reproductive decisions of American women. When I graduated from college in 1957, the average woman had 3.7 births. Today, they have 2.0 births. Demography is a fickle science, and it is anybody's guess whether American women will continue to have such low fertility rates. There are strong arguments that women, now increasingly incorporated into the work force, are finding exciting lifestyle alternatives to child-rearing. Unless there is a dramatic increase in U.S. fertility, we can look primarily to immigration as the factor standing between the U.S. and population stabilization.

The United States adds about 3 million people a year to our population of 250 million. Immigration, and the children of immigrants, account for more than half that growth. Under the new immigration law passed in 1990, we can anticipate that the immigrant population will grow substantially. Some experts expect that as many as 15 million people—the equivalent of two New York Cities—will settle in the United States during the 1990s.

In some areas of the country, like California, the impact of this influx will be acute. Demographer Leon Bouvier has projected that current immigration and natural increase patterns will result in California growing from 30 million in 1990 to 50 million residents by 2010. The state itself anticipates that it has to build the equivalent of a new school every single day to keep pace with the influx of children to California—clearly an impossible task. And this does not even begin to address the question of whether California, which already has severe pollution problems and suffers from a chronic shortage of water, could sustain a population of 50 million.

It is clear to me that it is in the best interest of our children and grandchildren to stabilize our own population and to assist other nations to do the same. We can do it ourselves, or nature will eventually do it for us—probably a lot less kindly. Public policy in the United States is struggling to resolve such problems as unemployment, crime, health care, education, poverty, pollution and national unity. All of these problems are aggravated by additional population growth.

It is axiomatic that developed nations like the United States create far more impact per capita on the environment and resources of the world than do people in the developing world. A person in the United States uses more than 30 times the energy resources as his counterpart in parts of Africa. Similarly, people in the developed regions have a greater impact on atmospheric carbon dioxide buildup, ozone depletion, soil erosion and ground water contamination. Our resource use greatly exceeds that of other world citizens. We may feel a warm glow of satisfaction by allowing an immigrant to enter the U.S., but that immigrant will soon be consuming his disproportionate share of world resources as well. In every way, we have set up unsustainable models of population growth and resource consumption.

I believe the best role for America is as a model—a sustainable society for the rest of the world to emulate. We must stabilize our population and reduce our disproportionate impact on the world's environment. This would require us to restrict immigration—not totally, but dramatically. America, in the 21st century, would be a much better "beacon" to the world if we developed new policies to face the world's new realities and urged other countries to follow us, rather than being a haven for a relative few abandoning their own countries. ❏

Migration No Longer the Answer

The conditions for unprecedented human migration from poorer to wealthier nations are unmistakably present. Human population now stands at 5.5 billion and is increasing by a quarter of a million people daily. Traditional ways of life in the less developed countries are being irrevocably disrupted by rapid urbanization. Job creation in those urban areas cannot begin to keep pace with the number of new workers entering the labor force. Modern communications have made even those in the remotest villages aware of the promise of a better life in other countries. And, modern transportation has made access to the wealthy, developed countries relatively easy.

To be sure, the aspirations of today's migrants are no different from those which have motivated people to move since the dawn of mankind. However, what was possible in a world which until 1800 had fewer than one billion people is no longer possible in one which is adding a billion people every 10 years. Nevertheless, the human urge to migrate in search of a better life persists and poses serious dilemmas for the developed nations to which immigrants are flocking.

The destination of choice for those who are on the move, or contemplating migration, is the United States. To millions around the world, the United States remains the land of opportunity, as it was for the millions of immigrants who preceded them to these shores. But unlike previous waves of immigrants who settled an open frontier and fueled an industrial revolution, today's immigrants arrive in a country that is already densely populated, with an elaborate social infrastructure, and which is struggling to keep its place in the post-industrial, sophisticated, and highly-com-

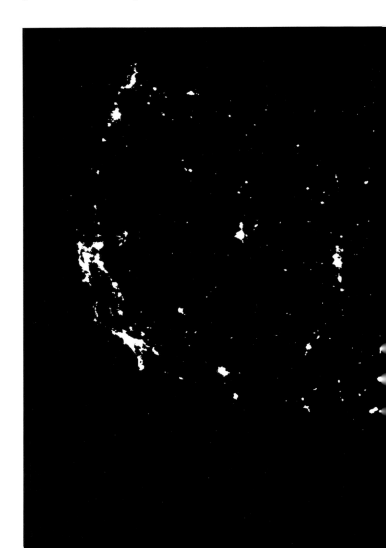

petitive global economy.

The United States, given its current population, population distribution and consumption of resources, is maintaining an existence that is unsustainable in the long term. In many areas of the country the United States is doing irreparable damage to its environment and robbing future generations of their resource base.

The following pages will demonstrate the patterns of population growth in the United States and the effect this growth is having on the environment. As global population continues to explode, the capacity of the United States to absorb immigrants will continue to diminish.

In the coming decades we will be faced with two irreconcilable phenomena: The human impulse to migrate in search of better conditions and the ecological limits to our absorptive capacity.

Population distribution patterns are evident in this U.S. night satellite view. Coastal regions including the mid and north Atlantic states, the Great Lakes and California are among the most crowded. The least crowded is the western interior where water is scarce and population size is necessarily limited.

The Dominance of North America

The United States is the world's largest consumer of energy and its most wasteful. Even the very wealthy countries of Europe consume only 60 percent as much energy on a per capita basis and the Japanese a mere 40 percent. By using an inordinate share of the world's nonrenewable resources, the United States is also contributing disproportionately to environmental pollution and to the greenhouse effect.

While per capita energy consumption has remained constant in the United States over the past 20 years, overall consumption has continued to rise because our population is growing faster than any other developed nation. These sustained high levels of per capita consumption and relative wealth make it extremely difficult, perhaps impossible, for developing nations to compete in the global market for the resources they will need to achieve economic parity with the developed countries.

This situation has led to a global Catch-22. Because those countries cannot meet the economic expectations of their people, migration to developed regions continues. However, in some cases, the migration of a single individual to the United States can result in as much as a 30-fold increase in energy consumption by that same person. In the case of large-scale migration, this seriously retards the ability of developing nations to aquire the resources they need, while simultaneously creating pressures in the United States to meet the demands of a growing population.

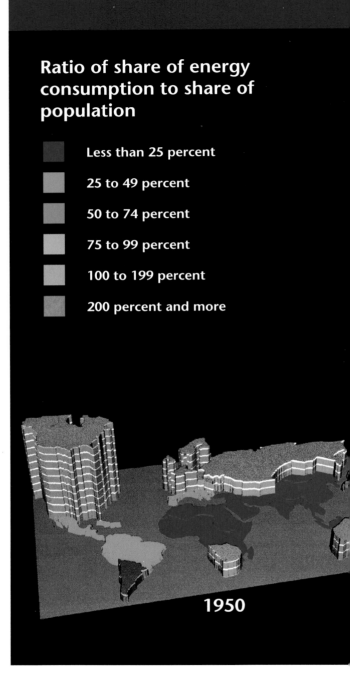

Ratio of share of energy consumption to share of population

- Less than 25 percent
- 25 to 49 percent
- 50 to 74 percent
- 75 to 99 percent
- 100 to 199 percent
- 200 percent and more

1950

During the 1980s, the U.S. population increased by approximately 22 million people. The additional energy consumption required to meet the demands of these new Americans would have served the energy

28

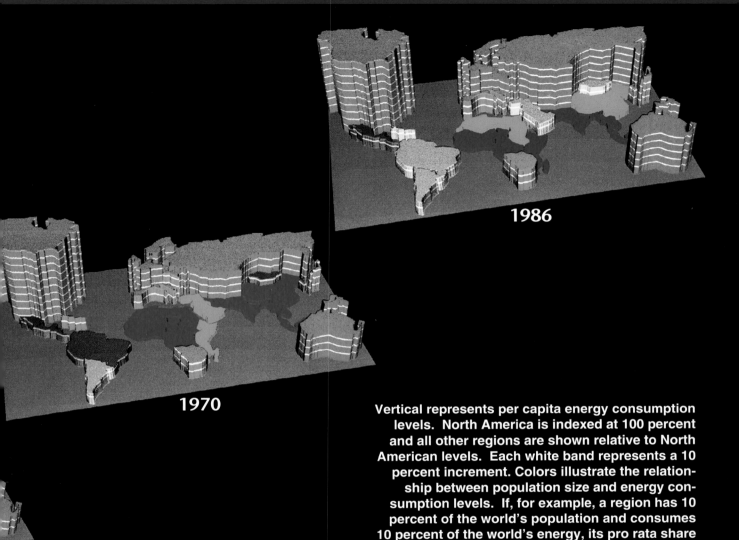

1986

1970

Vertical represents per capita energy consumption levels. North America is indexed at 100 percent and all other regions are shown relative to North American levels. Each white band represents a 10 percent increment. Colors illustrate the relationship between population size and energy consumption levels. If, for example, a region has 10 percent of the world's population and consumes 10 percent of the world's energy, its pro rata share is exactly 100 percent. A region with 5 percent of the population using 15 percent of the world's energy has a 300 percent pro rata share (and would be shown in red).

needs of 55 million Japanese; 150 million Tropical South Americans; 530 million West Africans; or 660 million Southern Asians.

29

Growth in Energy Consumption Due to Growth in Population

W ith the oil embargo of 1973, the U.S. public became painfully aware of its dependence on unreliable foreign energy sources. While the per capita consumption of energy in the U.S. grew precipitously during the 1950s and 1960s, the rate of per capita increase leveled off in the last 20 years. The aggregate consumption of energy, however, has continued to rise as population has grown by about 25 percent.

The United States has become much more efficient at using energy—although not nearly as efficient as the Europeans and Japanese. In 1987 it took 38 percent less energy to produce one dollar's worth of GNP than it did in 1973. Americans now consume 15 percent less gasoline to run automobiles despite the fact that the number of registered vehicles has grown by 20 percent.

In 1985, before the war in the Persian Gulf, the United States spent $47 billion on military activities in that region, which supplies less than 10 percent of our energy needs. Factoring in the military costs, Americans paid $468 per barrel of Persian Gulf oil. Had the U.S. simply stabilized its population, American reliance on energy from that part of the world could have been eliminated entirely.

1960

Per capita energy consumption in BTUs (millions)

- Less than 240
- 240 to 279
- 280 to 319

The nine U.S. regions are: New England, Middle Atlantic, South Atlantic, East-North Central, West-North Central, East-South Central, West-South Central, Mountain and Pacific (including Alaska and Hawaii).

Vertical represents total energy consumption by the nine U.S regions. Each white band represents 2 trillion BTUs. Colors represent per capita energy consumption levels.

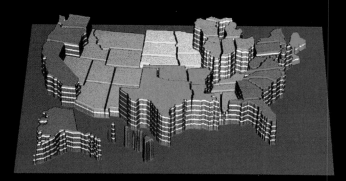

1973

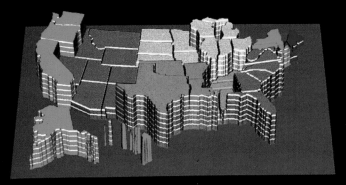

1988

320 to 359

360 to 399

400 and more

A Century of U.S. Population Growth

It should come as no surprise that the population of the United States has quadrupled in the last hundred years. U.S. population has grown at almost precisely the global rate over that period. By the standards of the developed world, our growth rate has been high, but by those of less developed countries it has been below the norm.

Two things distinguish U.S. population growth from that of most other countries, however. One is the high numbers of international immigrants it has absorbed and the other is the degree to which recent immigrants have affected regional shifts in population distribution.

During 1890 to 1930, U.S. population doubled from 63 million to 123 million people. Immigration was a primary factor in this growth as more than 20 million people entered the country during this period. Despite this enormous population growth, the distribution of the population changed very little. It continued to be concentrated in the northeast and around the Great Lakes. The immigrants settled primarily in the most densely populated regions, taking advantage of the existing economic and social infrastructure.

The years between 1930 and 1950 were a watershed period in U.S. history. Population, for a variety of reasons, grew only moderately for the only time this century. The virtual shut-off of immigration, the Great Depression, low birth rates and a world war all contributed to a hiatus in the otherwise steady and rapid pace of growth. During this period a new population distribution pattern began to emerge with marked growth in the southwestern and western part of the country.

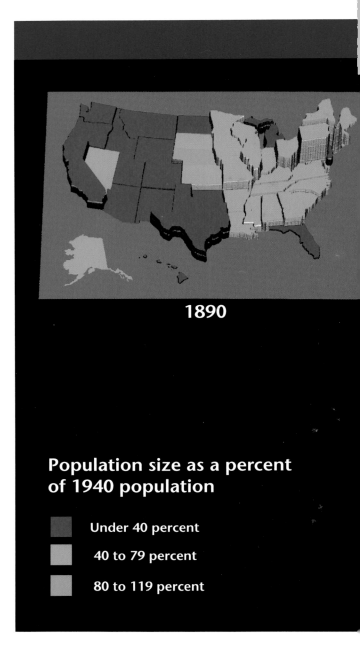

1890

Population size as a percent of 1940 population

- Under 40 percent
- 40 to 79 percent
- 80 to 119 percent

California, Texas and Florida accounted for 6 percent of the total U.S. population in 1890. In 1940, those same three states accounted for 11.5 percent of the U.S. population. Sixteen percent of all U.S. population growth over this 50-year period, a total of 11.4 million people, occurred in those states.

Vertical represents percent share of total U.S. population by state. Each white horizontal band is equal to 2 percent of the total U.S. population. Colors correspond to population size relative to 1940, which is indexed at 100 percent. Nebraska's 1890 population, for example, was nearly equal to its size in 1940 (and is shown in dark green).

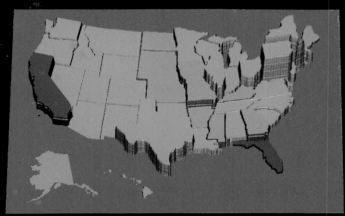

1910

1930

The Shift South and West

America's postwar era of unparalleled global dominance also saw a sharp upward surge in U.S. population after the slower growth of the previous two decades. U.S. population grew by more than 50 million people between 1950 and 1970, spurred by an unprecedented domestic baby boom. This 20-year span also saw the reemergence of immigration as a demographic force. It was also during these decades that the pattern of population shift to the south and west became clear. Largely through internal migration, new population centers, which relied on the automobile and the importation of water over great distances—such as Los Angeles—emerged as important metropolitan areas.

By 1970, the baby boom had ended and the nation was experiencing a protracted "baby bust." Nevertheless, over the next 20 years, the United States added another 50 million people to its population. This time the growth was in large measure the result of immigration which, by the end of the 1980s, had reached the highest levels in U.S. history.

The population redistribution shift that began in the aftermath of World War II was unmistakable. By 1990, California alone had as many people as there were in the entire United States at the time of the Civil War. The new population pattern was reinforced by continuing large scale immigration, as immigrants sought to take advantage of economic opportunities in these areas.

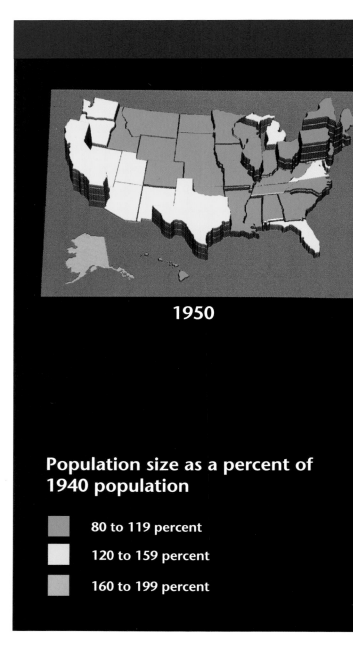

1950

Population size as a percent of 1940 population

- 80 to 119 percent
- 120 to 159 percent
- 160 to 199 percent

California, Texas and Florida, which accounted for 11.5 percent of the total U.S. population in 1940, accounted for 24 percent of the U.S. population in 1990. Thirty-eight percent of all U.S. population growth over this 50-year period, or 44.5 million people, occurred in those three states.

Vertical represents percent share of U.S. population by state. Each white horizontal band is equal to 2 percent of the total U.S. population. Colors correspond to population size relative to 1940, which is indexed at 100 percent. California's 1990 population, for example, is more than 300 percent its size in 1940 (and is shown in red).

1970

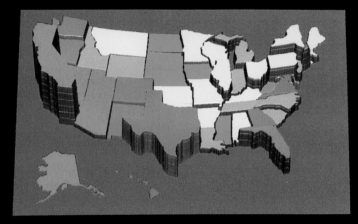

1990

- 200 to 299 percent
- 300 percent and more

A Century of Coastal Population Trends

For the first 150 years of U.S. history, population was concentrated in the coastal regions of the northeast and along the Great Lakes. Since the end of World War II, settlement patterns have changed dramatically. While the populations of the northeast and Great Lakes have remained relatively unchanged since 1940, there has been very rapid growth in Florida and along the southern Pacific coast. Both regions are ecologically fragile and are proving ill-suited to the enormous population pressures being placed on them.

Florida, and particularly the coastal regions of California, are prime destinations for new immigrants arriving in the United States. California alone settles one in four legal immigrants to the United States and almost one in two illegal immigrants. At current legal and illegal immigration levels, that amounts to more than 300,000 people annually. Immigration consequently has a direct and tangible impact on the population growth of America's crowded coastal counties. Moreover, there is no end in sight to the high levels of immigration Florida and California are experiencing.

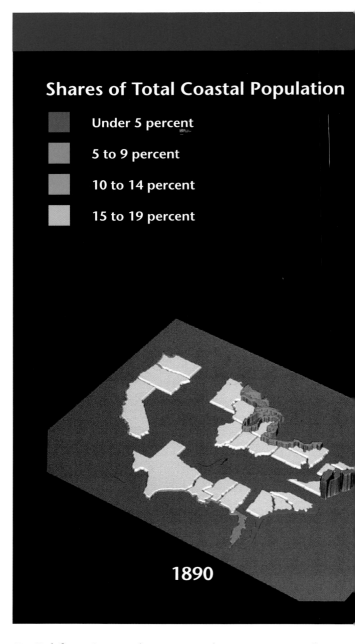

Shares of Total Coastal Population

- Under 5 percent
- 5 to 9 percent
- 10 to 14 percent
- 15 to 19 percent

1890

In California's coastal counties, where 80 percent of the state's population is concentrated, population density is currently just over 600 people per square mile. By 2010, when California's population is projected to reach 50 million, population density in the coastal areas would be 1,050 people per square mile.

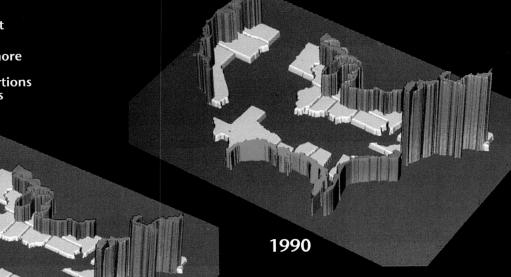

- 20 to 24 percent
- 25 percent or more
- Non-coastal portions of coastal states

1990

1940

Vertical represents population density per square mile for the 426 coastal counties of the continental United States (grouped into six regions). Colors represent percent shares of the total coastal county population. The six coastal regions are: 1) New England (including New York), 2) Northeast, 3) Southeast (Atlantic), 4) Gulf Coast, 5) Pacific, 6) Great Lakes.

The United States Coastal Population

A glance at a statistical table in an atlas would give the impression that the United States is a sparsely populated country, in comparison to most other nations. However, simple statistics are often misleading. *Along the coasts, where nearly half the population lives, the U.S. is among the more densely populated countries in the world.*

Forty-six percent of the U.S. population lives on just 10.5 percent of the continental land mass. These coastal regions also happen to be among the most ecologically sensitive areas in the country. With approximately 110 million people and much of our industry crammed on and around fragile wetlands and estuaries, the strain on the environment is intense.

Wetlands are an incubator for many species of plants and animals. They also are the ecosystem's natural filters, aiding in the breakdown of natural and man-made pollutants and contaminants. As population in these areas increases, many of these wetlands are irrevocably lost. *Ironically, as population grows and encroaches on wetlands, it destroys the ecological basis that supports all population.*

More than half the wetlands in the United States have already been lost. At the time of American independence there were more than 200 million acres of wetlands; today there are only 99 million acres left, and they are being debased or destroyed at a rate of 1,000 acres a day. Louisiana alone loses more than 25 square miles of coastal wetlands every year.

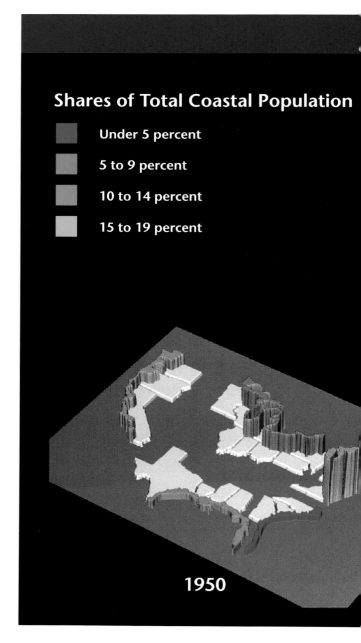

Shares of Total Coastal Population

- Under 5 percent
- 5 to 9 percent
- 10 to 14 percent
- 15 to 19 percent

1950

In 1990, the coastal region of the Northeast, including New England and New York, had a population density of 767 people per square mile. By comparison, El Salvador, the most densely populated

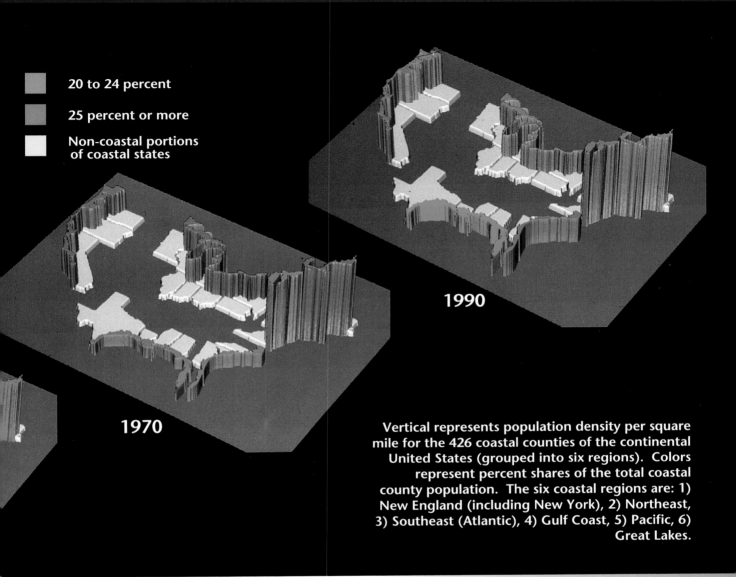

20 to 24 percent

25 percent or more

Non-coastal portions
of coastal states

1990

1970

Vertical represents population density per square mile for the 426 coastal counties of the continental United States (grouped into six regions). Colors represent percent shares of the total coastal county population. The six coastal regions are: 1) New England (including New York), 2) Northeast, 3) Southeast (Atlantic), 4) Gulf Coast, 5) Pacific, 6) Great Lakes.

nation overall in the Western Hemisphere had a density of 671. Haiti, the poorest country in the hemisphere, had a density of 580 people per square mile.

Visible in this late winter satellite image are the heavily silted tributaries—the Potomac, Rappahannock and James Rivers—indicative of the natural and man-made flow that washes into the Chesapeake.

The Chesapeake Bay—Population Pressure on Delicate Wetlands

The Chesapeake is the largest bay in the United States and serves as the watershed catch basin for a 64,000-square mile area from upstate New York to Southern Virginia. It is the hub of an enormous natural filtration system which traps both natural and man-made pollutants that flow from its many tributaries.

The Bay itself—195 miles long and 30 miles across at its widest—is actually the nexus of a watershed system 20 times as large. Nearly 50 significant rivers and thousands of smaller streams penetrate deep into the surrounding areas. Every drop of rain, as well as every pollutant discharged into this tributary system, eventually finds its way into the Chesapeake.

The extremely shallow and ecologically fragile Bay is easily damaged by upstream pollutants including fertilizers, pesticides and soil run-off. The Chesapeake contains less than one-tenth the volume of water relative to most other major coastal bays. Because of the Bay's tidal action, pollutants washed downstream remain in the Chesapeake for long periods of time.

The Chesapeake is also the largest estuary in the United States. The brackish mixture of fresh and salt water is nature's incubator for countless species of plant and marine life. Already, about 40 percent of the Bay's surrounding forests, particularly those along the water's edge, and more than half of the wetlands have been lost.

The population growth both along the Bay itself and along its upstream tributaries has placed enormous ecological stress on the Chesapeake. Since 1950, population has grown by 50 percent while energy consumption has doubled and air pollution has increased by more than 250 percent. These are among the many ripple effects of increased population.

In this satellite view, the expanding sprawl of Washington, D.C., and Baltimore, Maryland, the two major urban areas abutting the Chesapeake, is plainly evident. Also visible in this late winter satellite image are the heavily silted tributaries—the Potomac, Rappahannock and James Rivers—indicative of the natural and man-made flow that washes into the Chesapeake.

41

The Los Angeles Basin

The Los Angeles basin in southern California at the turn of the century was among the most promising agricultural regions in the nation. From fewer than 100,000 in 1890, population increased to 3 million in 1940. By 1990, it had surged to 11 million, becoming the nation's second largest metropolitan area. Increasingly, it is the destination point for immigrants. More than one million foreign born came to Los Angeles during the 1980s.

Now, urban buildup covers nearly the entire basin, as seen in this satellite image. Traffic congestion, noise, pollution, a deteriorating standard of living, growing violence and generally crowded conditions have replaced the irrigated orange groves and spaciousness that prevailed just one lifetime ago. Natural features have been permanently altered. Dams arrest the rivers, the sporadically flowing Los Angeles river is sealed in cement and the alluvial soil of the valley's floodplain is covered in concrete and buildings. Now, it is a "heat island."

In order to grow, Los Angeles from the very outset had to reach out great distances to gain water rights and electricity supplies. Its grasp quickly extended north to the Owens Valley. Shortly after, the aqueduct was extended another hundred miles to the Mono Basin. Both districts are on the eastern slopes of the High Sierras and have become the source of 80 percent of Los Angeles' water supply. Still another aqueduct extends due east to the Colorado River. Contentious and long standing legal battles rage among the southwestern states and between the United States and Mexico over water rights to the Colorado.

Water availability and distribution are the life blood of the southwestern United States. The entire region is essentially a desert. Los Angeles sustains its massive population only through modern engineering. Expansionist planning continues even today, as Los Angeles attempts to tap into Northern California's still abundant water supplies. This is tempered, however, by public recognition of ecological and environmental issues and consequences to habitat and by the realization that population stabilization may offer the far better long-term solution.

Further growth in the Los Angeles basin is nonetheless expected, fed largely by immigration. For many destined to arrive, it is still the "City of Dreams," even though the reality is tarnished.

42

43

Florida and its Everglades, the "River of Grass"

Florida's population grew from 400,000 to 13 million during the last century. In 1940—the midpoint—it was still just 1.9 million. A full 90 percent of the increase has come since then.

During this brief interval, human economic activities have severely disrupted the peninsula as it once existed. In its natural state, South Florida is characterized by free flowing rainwater draining back to the sea via a broad and inches-deep "river of grass." Nature's subtle relationships, however, have been brutally altered in the 20th century. Water impoundments and drainage canals, urban sprawl, large-scale agriculture, and cattle and horse ranching continue to destroy the natural endowment.

In its earlier natural state, water spilled periodically over the Lake Okeechobee southern rim, and spread as a 50 mile sheet across the saw grass, moving at about a hundred feet a day. The natural drainage combined with rainfall replenishment along the way nurtured and sustained the only tropical region in the continental United States.

At the turn of the century, businessmen and politicians began the drive to construct levees around Lake Okeechobee's southern rim to hold the water in and dig canals to regulate the flow. This was done to control periodic floods, provide drainage, foster agriculture and irrigation and sell urban real estate. The lake is now completely encircled by a dike, which constricts the heart of the free flowing system. By 1980, some 1,400 miles of canals and levees were carved out. A satellite image of the Loxahatchee Slough (inset), which is still preserved, shows one result—a vastly reduced water wilderness hard-pressed on the east by urban sprawl and on the west by agricultural fields.

Tampering with the system has produced enormous ecological and environmental problems that are nowhere near resolution. The portion of the Everglades drained for agriculture reveals a peaty muck that needs constant fertilization, pest and water level control. The drying muck itself shrinks a foot a year for a time. The result is compacted soil and fine blown dust that threatens to shrink back to bedrock level. North of the Lake, where cattle are raised, 1.5 tons of phosphorus waste flow into the lake daily and settle on its silty bottom. This speeds up the natural aging process of eutrophication and, eventually, to the biological death of the Lake itself.

Water use was once efficiently allocated by nature in the Everglades. It is the central resource in the entire system. It cannot be reconfigured over a long duration without carrying the seeds of its own destruction and it cannot be replaced. That simple fact is increasingly recognized. Yet, irreconcilable population pressures continue to be placed on it.

Bisected by the Columbia River, the Portland, Oregon metro area(lower left) is shown in this 105 by 90 mile image along with Mt. St. Helens and the wide swath of destruction caused by its explosion in 1980 (upper center). Also visible are the snow covered volcanoes of Mt. Adams (right center) and Mt. Hood (lower right).

Forest Loss in the Pacific Northwest

When European settlers first arrived on the North American continent, some 1.1 billion acres of land in what is now the United States were forested. Although today there are about 730 million acres of forested land, only about 10 percent of the original "old growth" stands still remain.

Nowhere is the battle to preserve what is left of the old growth forests more intense than in the Pacific Northwest. This satellite image shows the destruction of habitat as a result of forest clear cutting practices. Scores of clear cut tracts (in green) dot the forest floor amid the mountains and federally designated "wilderness" areas.

In recent years, the spotted owl has become a rallying point for those seeking to preserve old growth forests and a symbol of the destructive ripple effect caused by the loss of these ecosystems. Since 1930, the owl's old growth habitat has been reduced from 6 to 2 million acres. At stake is more than the fate of one particular species of owl. In its natural state, the forest supports an infinite variety of life forms ranging from fungus, beetles and insects found in fallen and rotting trees to the deer and other large animals that feed on new tree shoots. When it is destroyed, there is a chain reaction often felt beyond the forest itself.

The greatest effect is on the hydrological cycle. There is more fresh water stored in the world's forests than in all the world's lakes. Moisture emitted during the transpiration process and the evaporation of surface moisture collected on leaves is essential to the cycle. The evaporation feeds the rain clouds. Maintenance of the northwest forests is basic to the rain supply of the great agricultural belt far to the east.

The rate of forest destruction in the Pacific Northwest is gaining in intensity. According to a 1992 congressional committee report, reforestation efforts are lagging severely behind the rate at which the forests are being cut down. For every 100 acres being harvested, only 64 are being successfully reforested.

As U.S. population, pushed in part by rising immigration, continues to grow, the encroachment on private tract forests in the Pacific Northwest will grow commensurately. Forested tracts are forced to make way for suburban and exurban sprawl as communities spread out. Much more than trees, however, is sacrificed as poor choices are made between economic short-term benefits and the proper stewardship over an intrinsically valuable natural resource.

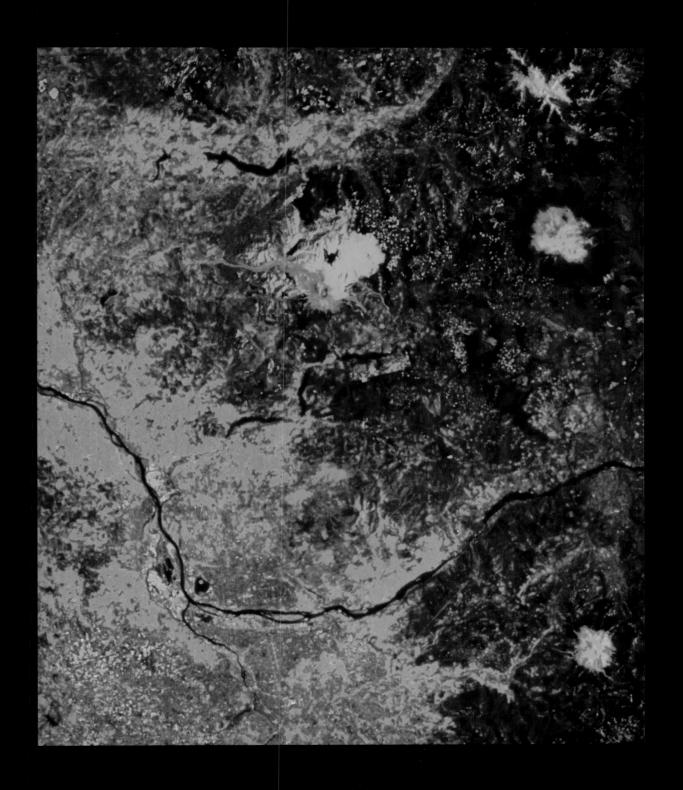

47

This satellite view shows hundreds of "center pivot" irrigation systems dotting the High Plains of western Kansas. The well-watered fields (in green) contrast sharply with the dry, brown surrounding soil.

Irrigation and Depletion of the Ogallala Aquifer

Beneath the High Plains of the central U.S. lies the Ogallala aquifer, a vast underground freshwater reservoir covering some 174,000 square miles, stretching from South Dakota to Texas (inset). The aquifer is the product of water deposited in gravel beds during the ice ages and stored there ever since. It is located beneath the American midwest, aptly named the "Great American Desert." Here, the rainfall is 20 inches a year, less as you move westward.

Circumstances changed in the 1920s with the invention of the centrifugal pump. It allows water to be brought to the surface at a rate of 800 gallons a minute or more, sufficient to irrigate over 100 acres, an area approximately the size of each of the hundreds of green circular fields irrigated by center-pivot systems. In 1980, some 170,000 irrigation wells were in operation on the High Plains.

The underground aquifer, however, is being depleted many times faster than it is replenished by precipitation and seepage from streams. It is estimated there were 3.25 billion acre feet of drainable water in 1980, down by 166 million acre feet since ground water development began. The U.S. Geological Survey notes the aquifer could be depleted by another five to six hundred million acre feet by 2020 based on current trends and water management scenarios.

One set of constraints to the future of the system is the cost of energy needed to pump water from a steadily falling water table, balanced against prices received from the sale of agricultural goods. The falling water table also decreases the rate at which water can be pumped, and consequently the acreage that can be irrigated.

The entire economy of this vast area now depends in large part on irrigated agriculture. Much of what is produced as food winds up in foreign markets to supply a rapidly expanding world population. Yet, while beneficial in the short run to agricultural interests and to the U.S. balance of trade, a precious non-renewable resource meanwhile is being mined and is literally draining away.

The ramifications extend far beyond simple economic cost and benefit analysis and into questions of the costs to the environment and a return to "dust bowl" conditions . Millions of acres, for example, might suddenly go fallow were irrigated farmland to go out of production due to aquifer depletion, rising energy pumping costs, a fall in commodity prices, or because of large personal debts incurred by farmers side by side with rising interest rates. Yet, water and crops are all that now hold the soil in place.

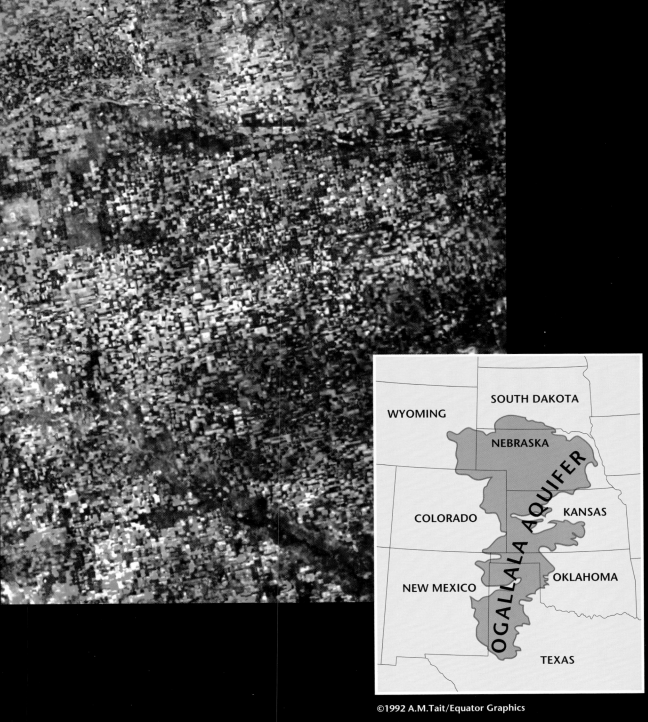

WYOMING

SOUTH DAKOTA

NEBRASKA

COLORADO

KANSAS

OGALLALA AQUIFER

NEW MEXICO

OKLAHOMA

TEXAS

©1992 A.M.Tait/Equator Graphics

49

TABLE 1 Population by World Region, 1950–2025

World regions are listed according to population growth rates—lowest (Western Europe, row 1) to highest (Eastern Africa, row 23)—as projected by the United Nations for the 35-year interval, 1990–2025. Population is in thousands.

Population is less than 2 times size in 1950

2 to 3 times size in 1950

3 to 4 times

4 to 5 times

5 to 6 times

6 times and more

		1950	1955	1960	1965
	World	2,516,443	2,752,107	3,019,653	3,336,319
	More Developed Regions	832,425	887,424	944,851	1,002,920
	Less Developed Regions	1,684,018	1,864,684	2,074,802	2,333,400
1	Western Europe	140,919	145,641	151,753	160,047
2	Southern Europe	109,014	113,675	118,197	123,529
3	Japan	83,625	89,815	94,096	98,881
4	Northern Europe	72,477	73,832	75,647	78,396
5	Eastern Europe	70,113	75,184	79,473	83,036
6	Northern America	166,075	181,742	198,663	214,076
7	Former U.S.S.R.	180,075	196,159	214,335	230,940
8	Other East Asia	33,006	34,011	39,995	45,940
9	China	554,760	609,005	657,492	729,191
10	Temperate South America	25,471	28,076	30,768	33,555
11	Oceania	12,647	14,151	15,782	17,516
12	Caribbean	17,045	18,627	20,446	22,693
13	Southeastern Asia	182,033	200,415	224,605	252,829
14	India	357,561	395,096	442,344	495,156
15	Tropical South America	86,123	100,344	116,474	135,310
16	Central America	37,241	43,093	50,456	59,285
17	Northern Africa	51,798	57,994	65,115	73,297
18	Southern Africa	15,736	17,639	19,892	22,623
19	Southern Asia (minus India)	123,842	136,713	153,956	174,744
20	Western Asia	42,432	48,575	55,856	64,133
21	Western Africa	63,150	70,754	80,173	91,628
22	Middle Africa	26,316	28,792	31,811	35,343
23	Eastern Africa	64,984	72,774	82,326	94,165

Statistics: UN Population Division, 1990 estimates and projections, medium variant series.

TABLE 2 Population Growth Rates by World Region, 1950–2025

World regions are listed according to population growth rates—lowest (Western Europe, row 1) to highest (Eastern Africa, row 23)—as projected by the United Nations for the 35-year interval, 1990–2025.

Growth rate is less than 25 percent of the world average for the period

25 to 74 percent of world average

75 to 124 percent

125 to 174 percent

175 to 224 percent

225 percent and more

		1950–55	1955–60	1960–65	1965–70
	World	1.8	1.9	2.0	2.1
	More Developed Regions	1.3	1.3	1.2	0.9
	Less Developed Regions	2.0	2.1	2.4	2.5
1	Western Europe	0.7	0.8	1.1	0.6
2	Southern Europe	0.8	0.8	0.9	0.8
3	Japan	1.4	0.9	1.0	1.1
4	Northern Europe	0.4	0.5	0.7	0.5
5	Eastern Europe	1.4	1.1	0.9	0.7
6	Northern America	1.8	1.8	1.5	1.1
7	Former U.S.S.R.	1.7	1.8	1.5	1.0
8	Other East Asia	0.6	3.3	2.8	2.5
9	China	1.9	1.5	2.1	2.6
10	Temperate South America	1.9	1.8	1.7	1.6
11	Oceania	2.3	2.2	2.1	2.0
12	Caribbean	1.8	1.9	2.1	1.9
13	Southeastern Asia	1.9	2.3	2.4	2.5
14	India	2.0	2.3	2.3	2.3
15	Tropical South America	3.1	3.0	3.0	2.7
16	Central America	2.9	3.2	3.2	3.2
17	Northern Africa	2.3	2.3	2.4	2.5
18	Southern Africa	2.3	2.4	2.6	2.5
19	Southern Asia (minus India)	2.0	2.4	2.5	2.7
20	Western Asia	2.7	2.8	2.8	2.8
21	Western Africa	2.3	2.5	2.7	2.8
22	Middle Africa	1.8	2.0	2.1	2.3
23	Eastern Africa	2.3	2.5	2.7	2.8

Statistics: UN Population Division, 1990 estimates and projections, medium variant series.

1970	1975	1980	1985	1990	1995	2000	2005	2010	2015	2020	2025	
3,697,849	4,079,023	4,448,037	4,851,433	5,292,195	5,770,286	6,260,800	6,739,230	7,204,343	7,659,858	8,091,628	8,504,223	
1,048,890	1,095,170	1,136,500	1,174,365	1,206,557	1,236,045	1,264,077	1,288,605	1,309,555	1,327,398	1,342,047	1,353,936	
2,648,959	2,983,853	3,311,537	3,677,068	4,085,638	4,534,241	4,996,722	5,450,625	5,894,787	6,332,461	6,749,581	7,150,287	
165,207	169,157	170,464	171,629	173,127	174,439	175,578	175,790	175,407	174,679	173,533	172,023	1
128,339	133,358	138,812	142,362	144,087	145,956	147,811	148,963	149,309	149,073	148,533	147,755	2
104,331	111,524	116,807	120,837	123,460	125,904	128,470	130,468	131,035	130,348	129,029	127,496	3
80,457	81,822	82,494	83,180	84,233	85,251	86,132	86,724	87,219	87,724	88,144	88,299	4
85,940	89,323	92,660	95,037	96,925	98,601	100,494	102,269	103,799	105,092	106,191	107,136	5
226,480	238,807	251,910	264,777	275,865	285,843	294,712	302,946	311,205	319,273	326,387	331,957	6
242,766	254,469	265,546	277,537	288,595	298,616	308,363	317,902	327,059	335,736	343,871	352,116	7
51,984	57,947	63,408	68,451	73,085	77,802	82,359	86,388	89,676	92,468	94,860	96,798	8
830,675	927,269	996,134	1,059,522	1,139,060	1,222,562	1,299,180	1,354,235	1,395,328	1,435,683	1,476,852	1,512,585	9
36,274	39,231	42,296	45,461	48,589	51,687	54,784	57,846	60,828	63,698	66,425	68,970	10
19,329	21,160	22,799	24,587	26,481	28,338	30,144	31,891	33,582	35,226	36,781	38,207	11
24,890	27,264	29,179	31,247	33,685	36,127	38,546	40,923	43,291	45,701	48,130	50,476	12
286,709	323,532	360,063	401,498	444,767	490,104	535,057	577,156	616,405	654,571	690,831	726,017	13
554,911	620,701	688,856	769,183	853,094	946,716	1,041,543	1,134,690	1,223,483	1,304,001	1,371,767	1,442,386	14
154,864	175,617	198,533	222,816	248,127	273,985	299,975	325,929	351,712	377,088	401,579	424,762	15
69,666	81,359	92,678	104,750	117,676	131,281	145,135	159,056	172,935	186,684	200,160	213,183	16
83,158	93,799	107,240	123,348	140,553	159,245	178,949	199,330	219,580	238,925	256,728	274,390	17
25,581	28,866	32,379	36,372	40,928	45,972	51,416	57,168	63,108	69,074	74,821	80,133	18
199,589	227,917	259,557	301,090	347,475	399,060	453,957	510,895	567,050	621,066	672,141	719,451	19
73,670	85,267	98,610	114,584	131,754	151,196	171,975	193,812	216,546	240,376	264,347	287,751	20
105,202	121,715	141,258	165,141	193,702	227,426	266,645	311,360	360,430	410,942	460,383	507,455	21
39,599	45,243	52,183	60,209	70,054	81,933	95,981	112,344	130,958	151,395	172,266	192,342	22
108,228	123,675	144,172	167,815	196,873	232,243	273,594	321,148	374,399	431,034	487,868	542,536	23

1970–75	1975–80	1980–85	1985–90	1990–95	1995–00	2000–05	2005–10	2010–15	2015–20	2020–25	
2.0	1.7	1.7	1.7	1.7	1.6	1.5	1.3	1.2	1.1	1.0	
0.9	0.7	0.7	0.5	0.5	0.5	0.4	0.3	0.3	0.2	0.2	
2.4	2.1	2.1	2.1	2.1	1.9	1.7	1.6	1.4	1.3	1.2	
0.5	0.2	0.1	0.2	0.2	0.1	0.0	0.0	-0.1	-0.1	-0.2	1
0.8	0.8	0.5	0.2	0.3	0.3	0.2	0.1	0.0	-0.1	-0.1	2
1.3	0.9	0.7	0.4	0.4	0.4	0.3	0.1	-0.1	-0.2	-0.2	3
0.3	0.2	0.2	0.3	0.2	0.2	0.1	0.1	0.1	0.1	0.0	4
0.8	0.7	0.5	0.4	0.3	0.4	0.4	0.3	0.2	0.2	0.2	5
1.1	1.1	1.0	0.8	0.7	0.6	0.6	0.5	0.5	0.4	0.3	6
0.9	0.9	0.9	0.8	0.7	0.6	0.6	0.6	0.5	0.5	0.5	7
2.2	1.8	1.5	1.3	1.2	1.1	0.9	0.7	0.6	0.5	0.4	8
2.2	1.4	1.2	1.5	1.4	1.2	0.8	0.6	0.6	0.6	0.5	9
1.6	1.5	1.4	1.3	1.2	1.2	1.1	1.0	0.9	0.8	0.8	10
1.8	1.5	1.5	1.5	1.4	1.2	1.1	1.0	1.0	0.9	0.8	11
1.8	1.4	1.4	1.5	1.4	1.3	1.2	1.1	1.1	1.0	1.0	12
2.4	2.1	2.2	2.1	1.9	1.8	1.5	1.3	1.2	1.1	1.0	13
2.2	2.1	2.2	2.1	2.1	1.9	1.7	1.5	1.3	1.0	1.0	14
2.5	2.5	2.3	2.2	2.0	1.8	1.7	1.5	1.4	1.3	1.1	15
3.1	2.6	2.5	2.3	2.2	2.0	1.8	1.7	1.5	1.4	1.3	16
2.4	2.7	2.8	2.6	2.5	2.3	2.2	1.9	1.7	1.4	1.3	17
2.4	2.3	2.3	2.4	2.3	2.2	2.1	2.0	1.8	1.6	1.4	18
2.7	2.6	3.0	2.9	2.8	2.6	2.4	2.1	1.8	1.6	1.4	19
2.9	2.9	3.0	2.8	2.8	2.6	2.4	2.2	2.1	1.9	1.7	20
2.9	3.0	3.1	3.2	3.2	3.2	3.1	2.9	2.6	2.3	2.0	21
2.7	2.9	2.9	3.0	3.1	3.2	3.2	3.1	2.9	2.6	2.2	22
2.7	3.1	3.0	3.2	3.3	3.3	3.2	3.1	2.8	2.5	2.1	23

Rounding of numbers may affect data/color correspondence.

51

TABLE 3 Urban Population by World Region, 1950-2025

World regions are listed according to population growth rates—lowest (Western Europe, row 1) to highest (Eastern Africa, row 23)—as projected by the United Nations for the 35-year interval, 1990-2025. Population is in thousands.

- Urban population is less than 2 times size in 1950
- 2 to 3 times size in 1950
- 3 to 4 times
- 4 to 5 times
- 5 to 6 times
- 6 times and more

		1950	1955	1960	1965
	World	733,828	859,443	1,031,510	1,183,942
	More Developed Regions	448,223	506,047	571,947	637,664
	Less Developed Regions	285,606	353,396	459,563	546,278
1	Western Europe	94,595	101,031	108,541	118,414
2	Southern Europe	48,604	53,382	58,442	65,072
3	Japan	42,063	49,847	58,810	66,547
4	Northern Europe	54,454	56,293	58,670	62,743
5	Eastern Europe	24,064	28,856	33,891	38,260
6	Northern America	106,105	121,739	138,877	154,092
7	Former U.S.S.R.	70,772	86,117	104,598	121,016
8	Other East Asia	9,441	11,053	14,508	18,799
9	China	60,969	80,715	124,892	132,711
10	Temperate South America	16,505	19,342	22,375	25,296
11	Oceania	7,754	9,035	10,458	11,998
12	Caribbean	5,757	6,703	7,828	9,521
13	Southeastern Asia	26,937	32,437	39,487	47,674
14	India	61,695	69,540	79,413	93,084
15	Tropical South America	31,706	41,537	53,721	69,145
16	Central America	14,809	18,619	23,573	29,853
17	Northern Africa	12,667	15,693	19,507	24,585
18	Southern Africa	5,972	7,014	8,286	9,629
19	Southern Asia (minus India)	15,221	18,982	23,893	29,908
20	Western Asia	10,129	13,752	18,396	24,477
21	Western Africa	6,457	8,653	11,637	15,499
22	Middle Africa	3,747	4,597	5,688	7,430
23	Eastern Africa	3,405	4,507	6,020	8,188

Statistics: UN Population Division, 1990 estimates and projections, medium variant series.

TABLE 4 Rural Population by World Region, 1950-2025

World regions are listed according to population growth rates—lowest (Western Europe, row 1) to highest (Eastern Africa, row 23)—as projected by the United Nations for the 35-year interval, 1990-2025. Population is in thousands.

- Rural population is less than 2 times size in 1950
- 2 to 3 times size in 1950
- 3 to 4 times
- 4 to 5 times
- 5 to 6 times
- 6 times and more

		1950	1955	1960	1965
	World	1,782,615	1,892,664	1,988,143	2,152,377
	More Developed Regions	384,202	381,377	372,904	365,256
	Less Developed Regions	1,398,412	1,511,288	1,615,239	1,787,122
1	Western Europe	46,324	44,610	43,212	41,633
2	Southern Europe	60,410	60,293	59,755	58,457
3	Japan	41,562	39,968	35,286	32,334
4	Northern Europe	18,023	17,539	16,977	15,653
5	Eastern Europe	46,049	46,328	45,582	44,776
6	Northern America	59,970	60,003	59,786	59,984
7	Former U.S.S.R.	109,303	110,042	109,737	109,924
8	Other East Asia	23,565	22,958	25,487	27,147
9	China	493,791	528,290	532,600	596,480
10	Temperate South America	8,966	8,734	8,393	8,259
11	Oceania	4,893	5,116	5,324	5,518
12	Caribbean	11,288	11,924	12,618	13,172
13	Southeastern Asia	155,096	167,978	185,118	205,155
14	India	295,866	325,556	362,931	402,072
15	Tropical South America	54,417	58,807	62,753	66,165
16	Central America	22,432	24,474	26,883	29,432
17	Northern Africa	39,131	42,301	45,608	48,712
18	Southern Africa	9,764	10,625	11,606	12,994
19	Southern Asia (minus India)	108,621	117,731	130,063	144,836
20	Western Asia	32,303	34,823	37,460	39,656
21	Western Africa	56,693	62,101	68,536	76,129
22	Middle Africa	22,569	24,195	26,123	27,913
23	Eastern Africa	61,579	68,267	76,306	85,977

Statistics: UN Population Division, 1990 estimates and projections, medium variant series.

1970	1975	1980	1985	1990	1995	2000	2005	2010	2015	2020	2025	
1,352,449	1,540,877	1,757,265	2,048,296	2,390,170	2,777,245	3,197,679	3,632,041	4,073,987	4,540,448	5,015,147	5,492,874	
698,643	753,998	798,743	840,713	875,469	909,865	946,227	983,164	1,020,063	1,055,990	1,088,643	1,117,099	
653,806	786,879	958,522	1,207,583	1,514,701	1,867,379	2,251,452	2,648,877	3,053,925	3,484,458	3,926,504	4,375,775	
125,786	131,702	134,314	136,554	139,358	142,222	145,147	147,469	149,400	150,840	151,730	152,124	1
71,964	78,314	84,743	90,182	94,674	99,368	104,070	108,218	111,644	114,430	116,760	118,672	2
74,294	84,413	88,995	92,658	95,040	97,424	99,782	102,000	103,229	103,262	103,146	102,111	3
66,315	68,270	69,133	69,914	71,130	72,478	73,858	75,116	76,401	77,691	78,857	79,729	4
42,508	47,991	52,981	57,008	60,704	64,314	68,112	71,855	75,403	78,708	81,736	84,505	5
167,147	176,348	186,217	197,396	207,401	217,520	227,715	238,261	249,559	261,304	272,057	281,283	6
137,651	152,700	167,162	180,817	189,895	198,201	208,138	219,756	232,831	247,073	260,651	274,030	7
25,121	31,245	37,850	44,582	50,941	56,958	62,536	67,483	71,667	75,275	78,518	81,355	8
144,537	160,425	195,370	273,385	380,803	499,077	614,514	710,192	782,538	854,731	927,185	995,477	9
28,240	31,492	34,897	38,394	41,845	45,248	48,616	51,915	55,099	58,187	61,143	63,926	10
13,673	15,148	16,226	17,382	18,700	20,060	21,480	22,992	24,612	26,268	27,909	29,498	11
11,351	13,491	15,479	17,610	20,043	22,516	24,993	27,459	29,941	32,508	35,132	37,729	12
57,894	71,245	86,571	107,471	132,824	162,942	197,214	234,532	273,771	315,482	358,376	402,418	13
109,616	132,272	158,851	192,064	230,269	278,674	336,542	404,079	480,806	564,681	648,265	737,155	14
86,411	106,279	129,229	154,472	180,974	208,054	235,160	262,001	288,323	314,601	340,390	365,247	15
37,626	46,657	56,014	66,325	77,631	89,793	102,513	115,632	129,222	143,031	156,904	170,638	16
29,926	35,655	42,816	51,436	62,695	76,278	91,596	108,545	126,635	145,012	163,198	181,981	17
11,125	13,241	15,627	18,751	22,465	26,743	31,517	36,694	42,178	47,860	53,576	59,123	18
37,825	47,811	59,906	77,192	97,888	122,710	153,931	191,008	233,224	278,865	326,768	375,716	19
31,817	40,761	50,794	65,665	82,609	101,348	120,920	141,249	162,268	184,134	206,757	229,526	20
20,679	27,579	36,387	47,918	62,962	82,169	106,132	135,608	170,599	209,632	251,205	294,165	21
9,782	12,620	16,098	20,558	26,458	34,089	43,727	55,666	69,907	86,276	104,046	122,328	22
11,162	15,218	21,605	30,560	42,860	59,061	79,466	104,311	134,730	170,598	210,841	254,138	23

1970	1975	1980	1985	1990	1995	2000	2005	2010	2015	2020	2025	
2,345,400	2,538,146	2,690,772	2,803,137	2,902,025	2,993,041	3,063,121	3,107,189	3,130,356	3,119,410	3,076,481	3,011,349	
350,247	341,172	337,757	333,652	331,088	326,180	317,850	305,441	289,492	271,408	253,404	236,837	
1,995,153	2,196,974	2,353,015	2,469,485	2,570,937	2,666,862	2,745,270	2,801,748	2,840,862	2,848,003	2,823,077	2,774,512	
39,421	37,455	36,150	35,075	33,769	32,217	30,431	28,321	26,007	23,839	21,803	19,899	1
56,375	55,044	54,069	52,180	49,413	46,588	43,741	40,745	37,665	34,643	31,773	29,083	2
30,037	27,111	27,812	28,179	28,420	28,480	28,688	28,468	27,806	27,086	25,883	25,385	3
14,142	13,552	13,361	13,266	13,103	12,773	12,274	11,608	10,818	10,033	9,287	8,570	4
43,432	41,332	39,679	38,029	36,221	34,287	32,382	30,414	28,396	26,384	24,455	22,631	5
59,333	62,459	65,693	67,381	68,464	68,323	66,997	64,685	61,646	57,969	54,330	50,674	6
105,115	101,769	98,384	96,720	98,700	100,415	100,225	98,146	94,228	88,663	83,220	78,086	7
26,863	26,702	25,558	23,869	22,144	20,844	19,823	18,905	18,009	17,193	16,342	15,443	8
686,138	766,844	800,764	786,137	758,257	723,485	684,666	644,043	612,790	580,952	549,667	517,108	9
8,034	7,739	7,399	7,067	6,744	6,439	6,168	5,931	5,729	5,511	5,282	5,044	10
5,656	6,012	6,573	7,205	7,781	8,278	8,664	8,899	8,970	8,958	8,872	8,709	11
13,539	13,773	13,700	13,637	13,642	13,611	13,553	13,464	13,350	13,193	12,998	12,747	12
228,815	252,287	273,492	294,027	311,943	327,162	337,843	342,624	342,634	339,089	332,455	323,599	13
445,295	488,429	530,005	577,119	622,825	668,042	705,001	730,611	742,677	739,320	723,502	705,231	14
68,453	69,338	69,304	68,344	67,153	65,931	64,815	63,928	63,389	62,487	61,189	59,515	15
32,040	34,702	36,664	38,425	40,045	41,488	42,622	43,424	43,713	43,653	43,256	42,545	16
53,232	58,144	64,424	71,912	77,858	82,967	87,353	90,785	92,945	93,913	93,530	92,409	17
14,456	15,625	16,752	17,621	18,463	19,229	19,899	20,474	20,930	21,214	21,245	21,010	18
161,764	180,106	199,651	223,898	249,587	276,350	300,026	319,887	333,826	342,201	345,373	343,735	19
41,853	44,506	47,816	48,919	49,145	49,848	51,055	52,563	54,278	56,242	57,590	58,225	20
84,523	94,136	104,871	117,223	130,740	145,257	160,513	175,752	189,831	201,310	209,178	213,290	21
29,817	32,623	36,085	39,651	43,596	47,844	52,254	56,678	61,051	65,119	68,220	70,014	22
97,066	108,457	122,567	137,255	154,013	173,182	194,128	216,837	239,669	260,436	277,027	288,398	23

TABLE 5 Births by World Region, 1950-2025

World regions are listed according to population growth rates—lowest to highest—as projected by the United Nations for 1990–2025. Statistics in the chart are average annual number of births (in thousands) in each of the 5 year intervals. Colors indicate the ratio (as a percentage) of a region's share of world births to share of world population.

- Share of births is less than 70 percent of share of population
- 70 to 89 percent
- 90 to 109 percent
- 110 to 129 percent
- 130 to 149 percent
- 150 percent and more

		1950-55	1955-60	1960-65	1965-70
	World	98,457	102,586	111,759	119,049
	More Developed Regions	19,424	19,779	19,566	18,359
	Less Developed Regions	79,033	82,808	92,192	100,690
1	Western Europe	2,503	2,590	2,822	2,732
2	Southern Europe	2,360	2,411	2,501	2,468
3	Japan	2,054	1,664	1,659	1,808
4	Northern Europe	1,222	1,248	1,378	1,374
5	Eastern Europe	1,841	1,748	1,423	1,448
6	Northern America	4,274	4,674	4,578	3,963
7	Former U.S.S.R.	4,943	5,188	4,917	4,238
8	Other East Asia	1,239	1,623	1,683	1,724
9	China	25,342	22,717	26,173	28,718
10	Temperate South America	745	804	852	864
11	Oceania	369	411	444	451
12	Caribbean	668	712	836	844
13	Southeastern Asia	8,423	9,484	10,128	11,039
14	India	16,575	18,185	19,656	21,072
15	Tropical South America	4,235	4,779	5,408	5,604
16	Central America	1,895	2,182	2,516	2,873
17	Northern Africa	2,680	2,913	3,282	3,537
18	Southern Africa	728	804	899	941
19	Southern Asia (minus India)	6,143	6,818	7,647	8,716
20	Western Asia	2,161	2,438	2,693	2,942
21	Western Africa	3,382	3,841	4,363	4,880
22	Middle Africa	1,274	1,398	1,549	1,728
23	Eastern Africa	3,473	3,901	4,394	4,977

Statistics: UN Population Division, 1990 estimates and projections, medium variant series.

TABLE 6 Deaths by World Region, 1950-2025

World regions are listed according to population growth rates—lowest to highest—as projected by the United Nations for 1990–2025. Statistics in the chart are average annual number of deaths (in thousands) in each of the 5 year intervals. Colors indicate the ratio (as a percentage) of a region's share of world deaths to share of world population.

- Share of deaths is less than 70 percent of share of population
- 70 to 89 percent
- 90 to 109 percent
- 110 to 129 percent
- 130 to 149 percent
- 150 percent and more

		1950-55	1955-60	1960-65	1965-70
	World	51,741	49,625	49,026	46,728
	More Developed Regions	8,681	8,516	8,761	9,436
	Less Developed Regions	43,061	41,109	40,265	37,292
1	Western Europe	1,642	1,691	1,767	1,878
2	Southern Europe	1,158	1,124	1,136	1,158
3	Japan	815	717	704	701
4	Northern Europe	812	822	863	890
5	Eastern Europe	810	726	697	761
6	Northern America	1,633	1,767	1,897	2,048
7	Former U.S.S.R.	1,729	1,558	1,602	1,847
8	Other East Asia	1,006	513	517	501
9	China	14,531	13,035	11,840	8,483
10	Temperate South America	281	289	312	331
11	Oceania	166	170	176	191
12	Caribbean	276	263	263	254
13	Southeastern Asia	4,660	4,625	4,480	4,335
14	India	9,396	9,072	9,079	9,173
15	Tropical South America	1,491	1,540	1,596	1,628
16	Central America	685	667	673	707
17	Northern Africa	1,354	1,358	1,423	1,452
18	Southern Africa	350	352	367	373
19	Southern Asia (minus India)	3,304	3,430	3,561	3,695
20	Western Asia	1,062	1,063	1,059	1,059
21	Western Africa	1,898	1,996	2,117	2,239
22	Middle Africa	776	790	818	842
23	Eastern Africa	1,939	2,005	2,087	2,191

Statistics: UN Population Division, 1990 estimates and projections, medium variant series.

1970-75	1975-80	1980-85	1985-90	1990-95	1995-00	2000-05	2005-10	2010-15	2015-20	2020-25	
122,202	120,508	128,177	137,415	146,097	149,549	148,753	148,003	148,186	146,250	145,256	
17,899	17,404	17,560	17,260	16,975	16,750	16,719	16,498	16,217	16,150	16,041	
104,303	103,104	110,617	120,155	129,122	132,800	132,034	131,505	131,969	130,100	129,215	
2,258	2,026	2,103	2,114	2,091	2,003	1,888	1,828	1,813	1,793	1,759	1
2,329	2,150	1,856	1,719	1,784	1,807	1,751	1,655	1,596	1,548	1,541	2
2,071	1,735	1,509	1,380	1,434	1,564	1,579	1,425	1,294	1,258	1,295	3
1,201	1,052	1,069	1,122	1,136	1,097	1,028	1,000	1,006	1,011	1,006	4
1,557	1,677	1,544	1,429	1,377	1,398	1,418	1,400	1,356	1,331	1,324	5
3,651	3,704	4,029	4,054	3,903	3,802	3,765	3,869	3,909	3,906	3,851	6
4,499	4,757	5,185	5,207	4,902	4,825	4,916	4,998	4,971	4,927	4,906	7
1,660	1,424	1,412	1,323	1,392	1,394	1,318	1,229	1,201	1,195	1,183	8
26,856	20,663	19,519	23,290	24,545	23,567	19,764	17,595	18,258	19,221	19,280	9
918	991	1,009	1,024	1,037	1,060	1,082	1,096	1,102	1,103	1,107	10
483	459	474	495	510	523	524	524	526	526	525	11
818	739	773	821	841	840	834	846	872	891	907	12
11,391	12,014	12,471	12,508	12,839	12,751	12,226	11,810	11,815	11,701	11,827	13
22,419	22,690	25,258	25,922	27,859	28,002	27,504	26,511	25,009	22,737	23,913	14
5,810	6,243	6,642	6,932	7,107	7,200	7,331	7,459	7,554	7,617	7,642	15
3,215	3,135	3,301	3,453	3,580	3,658	3,722	3,781	3,845	3,905	3,945	16
3,798	4,162	4,612	4,872	5,131	5,317	5,458	5,460	5,291	5,052	5,122	17
1,014	1,091	1,187	1,300	1,397	1,478	1,540	1,592	1,611	1,596	1,541	18
9,908	11,132	12,623	13,526	14,722	15,267	15,636	15,544	14,907	14,555	13,924	19
3,178	3,530	3,965	4,436	4,855	5,144	5,422	5,695	5,977	6,100	6,095	20
5,567	6,399	7,423	8,638	9,844	11,131	12,419	13,400	13,739	13,527	13,002	21
1,951	2,221	2,550	2,981	3,455	3,955	4,475	4,961	5,365	5,442	5,279	22
5,681	6,583	7,497	8,815	10,242	11,545	12,894	14,182	14,904	14,995	14,560	23

1970-75	1975-80	1980-85	1985-90	1990-95	1995-00	2000-05	2005-10	2010-15	2015-20	2020-25	
47,078	47,265	48,079	49,650	50,891	51,858	53,086	54,936	57,306	59,645	63,612	
9,968	10,487	11,091	11,665	11,724	11,875	12,380	12,990	13,316	13,881	14,289	
37,111	36,778	36,989	37,984	39,167	39,983	40,706	41,946	43,990	45,764	49,324	
1,901	1,886	1,940	1,941	1,893	1,828	1,920	1,956	2,002	2,081	2,114	1
1,204	1,225	1,251	1,361	1,407	1,425	1,514	1,596	1,641	1,652	1,689	2
712	696	725	855	948	1,056	1,178	1,308	1,425	1,517	1,603	3
909	937	928	963	949	934	925	922	918	941	988	4
843	931	1,011	1,060	1,040	1,016	1,065	1,089	1,100	1,101	1,123	5
2,093	2,085	2,195	2,351	2,443	2,554	2,629	2,733	2,837	3,002	3,259	6
2,138	2,599	2,905	3,000	2,906	2,883	3,006	3,192	3,247	3,296	3,271	7
466	384	395	418	447	483	526	582	644	722	794	8
7,635	6,920	6,883	7,360	7,788	8,192	8,754	9,347	10,049	10,921	12,106	9
342	348	357	381	406	432	462	492	521	551	592	10
198	193	194	207	219	231	242	255	268	284	311	11
247	243	248	260	269	276	286	303	320	352	384	12
4,386	4,369	3,954	3,761	3,782	3,738	3,779	3,937	4,129	4,438	4,816	13
9,273	9,089	9,244	9,154	9,167	8,937	8,806	8,719	8,842	9,095	9,846	14
1,624	1,676	1,727	1,820	1,894	1,981	2,084	2,254	2,421	2,674	2,965	15
715	686	690	699	721	745	805	862	970	1,083	1,239	16
1,466	1,444	1,449	1,422	1,406	1,384	1,379	1,402	1,443	1,486	1,592	17
380	385	391	394	390	389	390	402	423	446	480	18
4,010	4,009	4,155	4,222	4,307	4,398	4,372	4,327	4,154	4,394	4,237	19
1,038	972	1,020	1,044	1,044	1,048	1,095	1,147	1,232	1,311	1,407	20
2,388	2,557	2,734	2,951	3,148	3,324	3,486	3,618	3,656	3,654	3,625	21
876	928	987	1,033	1,099	1,153	1,205	1,249	1,281	1,276	1,256	22
2,325	2,510	2,846	2,981	3,122	3,277	3,438	3,537	3,615	3,623	3,653	23

TABLE 7 Women Ages 15-49 by World Region, 1950-2025

World regions are listed according to population growth rates—lowest (Western Europe, row 1) to highest (Eastern Africa, row 23)—as projected by the United Nations for the 35-year interval, 1990-2025. The number of women is in thousands.

	Number of women ages 15–49 is less than 1.75 times size in 1950
	1.75 to 2.4 times size in 1950
	2.5 to 3.24 times
	3.25 to 3.9 times
	4.0 to 4.74 times
	4.75 times and more

		1950	1955	1960	1965
	World	623,196	665,208	706,435	766,689
	More Developed Regions	223,824	232,360	235,549	246,356
	Less Developed Regions	399,373	432,848	470,886	520,333
1	Western Europe	36,775	36,571	35,975	36,581
2	Southern Europe	29,040	29,934	30,141	30,957
3	Japan	21,392	23,381	25,391	28,014
4	Northern Europe	18,241	17,886	17,700	18,076
5	Eastern Europe	19,227	19,619	19,546	20,407
6	Northern America	42,356	43,695	45,872	49,493
7	Former U.S.S.R.	54,303	58,600	58,007	59,583
8	Other East Asia	7,673	8,521	9,470	10,467
9	China	134,010	138,139	144,441	157,417
10	Temperate South America	6,560	7,090	7,598	8,181
11	Oceania	3,051	3,292	3,602	4,013
12	Caribbean	4,051	4,373	4,750	5,188
13	Southeastern Asia	43,998	48,369	53,012	58,227
14	India	83,968	93,319	103,112	113,546
15	Tropical South America	20,485	23,258	26,273	30,170
16	Central America	8,520	9,684	11,151	12,786
17	Northern Africa	12,127	13,459	14,788	16,091
18	Southern Africa	3,774	4,172	4,636	5,224
19	Southern Asia (minus India)	27,532	30,411	33,438	37,385
20	Western Asia	9,922	11,073	12,324	13,940
21	Western Africa	14,701	16,525	18,634	21,048
22	Middle Africa	6,446	7,032	7,708	8,464
23	Eastern Africa	15,046	16,805	18,867	21,431

Statistics: UN Population Division, 1990 estimates and projections, medium variant series.

TABLE 8 Fertility Rates by World Region, 1950-2025

World regions are listed according to population growth rates—lowest (Western Europe, row 1) to highest (Eastern Africa, row 23)—as projected by the United Nations for the 35-year interval, 1990-2025. The total fertility rate represents the average number of children a woman will bear on completion of her childbearing years under prevailing age-specific fertility rate conditions.

	Total fertility rate (TFR) is below 2.6 children per woman on average
	TFR in a range from 2.6 to 3.6
	3.7 to 4.7
	4.8 to 5.8
	5.9 to 6.9
	7 or more children

		1950-55	1955-60	1960-65	1965-70
	World	5.0	4.9	5.0	4.9
	More Developed Regions	2.8	2.8	2.7	2.4
	Less Developed Regions	6.2	6.0	6.1	6.0
1	Western Europe	2.4	2.5	2.7	2.5
2	Southern Europe	2.7	2.6	2.7	2.7
3	Japan	2.8	2.1	2.0	2.0
4	Northern Europe	2.3	2.6	2.8	2.5
5	Eastern Europe	3.0	2.7	2.3	2.4
6	Northern America	3.5	3.7	3.3	2.5
7	Former U.S.S.R.	2.8	2.8	2.5	2.4
8	Other East Asia	5.2	6.0	5.5	4.9
9	China	6.2	5.4	5.9	6.0
10	Temperate South America	3.5	3.5	3.6	3.3
11	Oceania	3.8	4.1	3.9	3.5
12	Caribbean	5.2	5.1	5.5	5.0
13	Southeastern Asia	6.0	6.1	5.9	5.8
14	India	6.0	5.9	5.8	5.7
15	Tropical South America	6.4	6.4	6.4	5.6
16	Central America	6.8	6.8	6.8	6.7
17	Northern Africa	6.8	7.0	7.1	6.9
18	Southern Africa	6.5	6.5	6.5	5.9
19	Southern Asia (minus India)	6.6	6.6	6.5	6.5
20	Western Asia	6.8	6.7	6.5	6.3
21	Western Africa	6.8	6.8	6.9	6.9
22	Middle Africa	5.9	5.9	6.0	6.0
23	Eastern Africa	6.8	6.8	6.9	6.9

Statistics: UN Population Division, 1990 estimates and projections, medium variant series.

	1970	1975	1980	1985	1990	1995	2000	2005	2010	2015	2020	2025	
	857,702	951,734	1,062,021	1,188,780	1,319,564	1,444,055	1,567,880	1,687,498	1,814,397	1,928,444	2,021,849	2,105,846	
	263,336	275,504	286,193	295,868	302,521	310,019	311,771	308,875	303,332	297,255	293,752	291,119	
	594,366	676,230	775,829	892,912	1,017,043	1,134,035	1,256,109	1,378,622	1,511,065	1,631,189	1,728,098	1,814,727	
	38,857	40,045	41,668	43,161	43,124	42,706	41,864	40,756	39,304	37,163	35,194	34,171	1
	31,818	32,695	33,878	34,939	36,009	36,795	36,482	35,688	34,696	33,299	31,761	30,213	2
	29,704	30,384	30,624	30,806	31,468	30,994	29,276	28,097	27,693	27,433	26,867	25,439	3
	18,176	18,438	19,240	20,238	20,875	20,836	20,347	20,258	20,040	19,361	18,633	18,216	4
	22,216	22,904	22,812	23,026	23,703	24,929	25,197	24,728	24,311	24,521	24,590	24,365	5
	54,187	59,513	65,217	69,627	72,828	74,721	75,309	74,660	72,794	70,866	70,303	70,677	6
	64,761	67,504	68,325	69,171	69,173	73,429	77,534	78,824	78,582	78,681	80,486	82,120	7
	11,804	13,913	16,078	18,577	20,698	22,099	23,028	23,611	23,564	23,463	22,826	21,980	8
	183,562	206,008	236,850	275,991	312,009	333,380	345,578	355,989	371,570	375,436	360,401	342,625	9
	8,882	9,626	10,326	11,058	11,927	12,892	13,778	14,538	15,218	15,862	16,507	17,026	10
	4,491	5,010	5,553	6,183	6,806	7,278	7,647	7,986	8,279	8,547	8,743	8,920	11
	5,600	6,290	7,146	8,022	8,876	9,445	10,002	10,641	11,237	11,509	11,705	11,954	12
	66,010	76,078	86,746	99,543	113,523	128,060	143,514	156,950	168,651	178,504	185,045	189,034	13
	126,291	141,903	159,836	179,925	202,321	225,602	253,492	281,186	310,408	337,399	360,647	379,063	14
	35,299	41,385	48,597	55,954	63,434	71,509	79,429	86,746	93,344	98,823	104,026	108,862	15
	15,102	17,825	21,144	25,025	29,640	33,907	38,383	42,604	46,544	49,940	52,654	54,649	16
	18,400	21,135	24,558	28,458	32,866	38,313	44,457	50,409	56,437	62,565	68,356	73,550	17
	5,964	6,865	7,884	8,946	10,111	11,382	12,806	14,374	16,029	17,694	19,420	21,099	18
	42,555	49,327	57,295	66,417	77,720	90,900	107,663	124,730	142,641	160,972	178,725	194,745	19
	16,310	19,102	22,034	25,803	30,104	34,995	40,523	46,717	53,398	60,075	66,839	73,478	20
	23,943	27,550	31,848	36,906	42,947	50,314	59,446	70,590	83,677	98,782	115,942	134,298	21
	9,369	10,541	11,976	13,702	15,819	18,389	21,461	25,226	29,831	35,293	41,625	48,732	22
	24,404	27,692	32,387	37,308	43,596	51,191	60,672	72,195	86,154	102,257	120,543	140,606	23

	1970-75	1975-80	1980-85	1985-90	1990-95	1995-00	2000-05	2005-10	2010-15	2015-20	2020-25	
	4.5	3.8	3.6	3.5	3.3	3.1	3.0	2.8	2.6	2.4	2.3	
	2.2	2.0	1.9	1.9	1.9	1.9	1.9	1.9	1.9	1.9	1.9	
	5.4	4.5	4.2	3.9	3.7	3.5	3.2	2.9	2.7	2.5	2.3	
	1.9	1.6	1.6	1.6	1.6	1.7	1.7	1.8	1.8	1.8	1.8	1
	2.5	2.3	1.8	1.6	1.6	1.7	1.7	1.7	1.8	1.8	1.8	2
	2.1	1.8	1.8	1.7	1.7	1.8	1.8	1.8	1.8	1.8	1.8	3
	2.1	1.8	1.8	1.8	1.8	1.8	1.9	1.9	1.9	1.9	1.9	4
	2.2	2.3	2.1	2.0	1.9	1.9	1.9	1.9	1.9	1.9	1.9	5
	2.0	1.9	1.8	1.8	1.8	1.9	1.9	1.9	1.9	1.9	1.9	6
	2.4	2.3	2.4	2.4	2.3	2.3	2.2	2.2	2.1	2.1	2.1	7
	4.5	3.3	2.9	2.5	2.3	2.2	2.1	2.1	2.0	2.0	1.9	8
	4.8	2.9	2.4	2.5	2.3	2.1	1.9	1.8	1.8	1.8	1.8	9
	3.2	3.2	3.1	3.0	2.8	2.6	2.5	2.4	2.3	2.2	2.2	10
	3.2	2.8	2.6	2.5	2.4	2.3	2.3	2.2	2.1	2.1	2.0	11
	4.4	3.5	3.2	3.0	2.9	2.8	2.7	2.7	2.6	2.6	2.6	12
	5.3	4.8	4.3	3.7	3.3	3.0	2.6	2.4	2.2	2.1	2.1	13
	5.4	4.8	4.8	4.3	4.1	3.7	3.3	2.9	2.5	2.1	2.1	14
	5.0	4.5	4.1	3.7	3.4	3.1	2.9	2.7	2.6	2.5	2.4	15
	6.3	5.1	4.5	3.9	3.5	3.1	2.9	2.7	2.6	2.5	2.5	16
	6.4	6.0	5.7	5.1	4.6	4.1	3.6	3.2	2.8	2.4	2.3	17
	5.6	5.2	5.0	4.7	4.4	4.1	3.8	3.5	3.1	2.8	2.4	18
	6.3	5.8	5.6	5.2	4.9	4.5	4.1	3.6	3.2	2.8	2.7	19
	6.0	5.6	5.4	5.1	4.7	4.3	4.0	3.6	3.3	3.0	2.7	20
	6.9	6.9	6.9	6.9	6.7	6.4	5.9	5.3	4.5	3.7	3.1	21
	6.1	6.2	6.2	6.2	6.2	6.1	5.9	5.5	5.0	4.3	3.5	22
	7.0	7.1	6.9	6.9	6.8	6.4	6.0	5.5	4.8	4.1	3.4	23

Rounding of numbers may affect data/color correspondence.

TABLE 9 Proportions of Children by World Region, 1950–2025

World regions are listed according to population growth rates—lowest to highest—as projected by the United Nations for the 35-year interval, 1990–2025. Statistics in the chart show the percentage of the total population under age 15.

Legend:
- Children (0–14) comprise less than 20 percent of the total population
- 20 to 24 percent
- 25 to 29 percent
- 30 to 34 percent
- 35 to 39 percent
- 40 percent and more

		1950	1955	1960	1965
	World	35	36	37	38
	More Developed Regions	28	28	29	28
	Less Developed Regions	38	39	41	42
1	Western Europe	23	23	24	24
2	Southern Europe	28	27	27	27
3	Japan	35	34	30	26
4	Northern Europe	23	24	24	24
5	Eastern Europe	28	28	29	27
6	Northern America	27	30	31	31
7	Former U.S.S.R.	30	28	31	31
8	Other East Asia	41	40	42	43
9	China	34	37	39	40
10	Temperate South America	32	32	33	33
11	Oceania	30	32	33	33
12	Caribbean	39	39	40	40
13	Southeastern Asia	39	40	41	43
14	India	39	39	40	40
15	Tropical South America	42	43	44	45
16	Central America	44	45	45	47
17	Northern Africa	41	42	43	45
18	Southern Africa	39	40	41	42
19	Southern Asia (minus India)	39	40	42	44
20	Western Asia	40	41	42	43
21	Western Africa	44	44	45	45
22	Middle Africa	41	42	42	43
23	Eastern Africa	44	44	45	45

Statistics: UN Population Division, 1990 estimates and projections, medium variant series.

TABLE 10 Population in Broad Age Groups (in thousands)

		1950	1955	1960	1965
World	total	2,516,443	2,752,107	3,019,653	3,336,319
	0 to 14	869,437	980,951	1,116,594	1,256,192
	15 to 64	1,519,198	1,628,026	1,742,988	1,902,486
	65 and over	127,807	143,133	160,067	177,641
More Developed Regions	total	832,425	887,424	944,851	1,002,920
	0 to 14	231,264	245,484	269,813	279,258
	15 to 64	537,595	570,051	594,789	633,065
	65 and over	63,566	71,887	80,250	90,597
Less Developed Regions	total	1,684,018	1,864,684	2,074,801	2,333,400
	0 to 14	638,175	735,465	846,783	976,933
	15 to 64	981,600	1,057,973	1,148,201	1,269,422
	65 and over	64,242	71,245	79,817	87,044

Statistics: UN Population Division, 1990 estimates and projections, medium variant series.

TABLE 11 Percent Distribution of Population in Broad Age Groups

World	0 to 14	35	36	37	38
	15 to 64	60	59	58	57
	65 and over	5	5	5	5
More Developed Regions	0 to 14	28	28	29	28
	15 to 64	65	64	63	63
	65 and over	8	8	8	9
Less Developed Regions	0 to 14	38	39	41	42
	15 to 64	58	57	55	54
	65 and over	4	4	4	4

Statistics: UN Population Division, 1990 estimates and projections, medium variant series.

1970	1975	1980	1985	1990	1995	2000	2005	2010	2015	2020	2025	
38	37	35	33	32	32	31	30	29	27	26	25	
27	25	23	22	21	21	20	19	19	19	18	18	
42	41	39	37	36	35	34	33	31	29	27	26	
24	23	20	18	18	18	18	17	16	16	16	16	1
27	26	24	22	20	18	18	18	17	17	16	16	2
24	24	24	22	18	17	17	17	17	16	15	15	3
24	23	21	20	19	19	19	19	18	17	17	17	4
25	24	24	24	23	22	21	20	20	20	19	19	5
28	25	23	22	21	21	20	19	18	18	18	18	6
29	26	25	25	25	25	24	23	22	22	21	21	7
43	39	35	31	27	25	24	23	22	20	19	18	8
40	39	35	30	26	26	27	24	21	19	18	19	9
32	31	31	30	30	29	28	27	26	25	24	24	10
32	31	29	28	27	26	25	24	23	22	21	21	11
41	40	36	33	31	31	30	29	27	26	26	25	12
43	43	41	39	37	35	33	31	28	26	24	23	13
40	40	39	38	36	36	34	33	30	28	25	23	14
43	41	39	38	36	35	33	31	29	28	27	26	15
47	46	44	42	39	37	35	33	31	29	28	27	16
45	44	43	42	41	40	38	36	34	31	29	27	17
41	41	39	39	38	38	37	36	34	33	31	29	18
45	45	44	44	44	43	41	39	36	33	30	28	19
43	43	42	41	40	40	39	37	36	34	32	31	20
46	46	46	46	47	47	47	46	45	42	40	36	21
43	44	45	45	45	46	46	46	45	44	42	38	22
46	46	46	47	47	47	47	46	45	43	41	37	23

Rounding of numbers may affect data/color correspondence.

1970	1975	1980	1985	1990	1995	2000	2005	2010	2015	2020	2025
3,697,849	4,079,023	4,448,037	4,851,433	5,292,195	5,770,286	6,260,799	6,739,230	7,204,343	7,659,858	8,091,628	8,504,223
1,386,957	1,504,616	1,566,235	1,624,624	1,710,393	1,848,134	1,966,950	2,037,527	2,063,913	2,074,772	2,079,600	2,085,212
2,110,756	2,342,665	2,617,827	2,936,768	3,254,169	3,547,432	3,869,335	4,225,741	4,616,690	4,987,282	5,304,215	5,590,847
200,138	231,741	263,985	290,039	327,634	374,720	424,516	475,964	523,739	597,805	707,813	828,164
1,048,890	1,095,170	1,136,500	1,174,365	1,206,557	1,236,045	1,264,077	1,288,605	1,309,555	1,327,398	1,342,047	1,353,936
278,863	271,551	263,014	259,759	257,373	255,749	252,550	249,871	247,932	245,708	243,265	241,107
669,016	706,087	742,626	779,848	803,571	819,827	838,710	853,087	868,227	870,953	865,783	855,806
101,007	117,535	130,858	134,754	145,614	160,468	172,819	185,645	193,398	210,734	232,998	257,026
2,648,959	2,983,853	3,311,537	3,677,068	4,085,638	4,534,241	4,996,722	5,450,625	5,894,787	6,332,461	6,749,581	7,150,287
1,108,093	1,233,066	1,303,220	1,364,866	1,453,020	1,592,384	1,714,400	1,787,656	1,815,980	1,829,064	1,836,335	1,844,105
1,441,736	1,636,580	1,875,199	2,156,917	2,450,599	2,727,605	3,030,625	3,372,649	3,748,465	4,116,329	4,438,435	4,735,046
99,128	114,208	133,128	155,285	182,018	214,252	251,696	290,318	330,341	387,068	474,813	571,136

1970	1975	1980	1985	1990	1995	2000	2005	2010	2015	2020	2025
38	37	35	33	32	32	31	30	29	27	26	25
57	57	59	61	61	61	62	63	64	65	66	66
5	6	6	6	6	6	7	7	7	8	9	10
27	25	23	22	21	21	20	19	19	19	18	18
64	64	65	66	67	66	66	66	66	66	65	63
10	11	12	11	12	13	14	14	15	16	17	19
42	41	39	37	36	35	34	33	31	29	27	26
54	55	57	59	60	60	61	62	64	65	66	66
4	4	4	4	4	5	5	5	6	6	7	8

TABLE 12 Population of the United States, 1890–1990

The 50 states and the District of Columbia are ranked in order of population growth rates—lowest to highest—for the overall period 1940–1990. Statistics show population in thousands. Colors indicate population in former years as a percentage of the 1990 population size. Washington, D.C. (row 1) in 1890, for example, was 38 percent (orange) its 1990 size.

- ■ Population is 85 percent or more of its size in 1990
- ■ 70 to 84 percent size in 1950
- ■ 55 to 69 percent
- □ 40 to 54 percent
- ■ 25 to 39 percent
- ■ Less than 25 percent

	1890	1900	1910	1920	1930	1940	1950	1960	1970	1980	1990
U.S. Total	62,721	76,747	92,198	106,005	123,197	132,184	151,291	179,420	203,302	226,546	248,710
Washington, D.C.	230	279	331	438	487	663	802	764	757	638	607
West Virginia	763	959	1,221	1,464	1,729	1,902	2,006	1,860	1,744	1,950	1,793
North Dakota	176	325	577	647	681	642	620	632	618	653	639
South Dakota	328	386	577	635	691	641	654	682	666	691	696
Iowa	1,912	2,232	2,225	2,404	2,471	2,538	2,621	2,757	2,825	2,914	2,777
Mississippi	1,290	1,551	1,797	1,791	2,010	2,184	2,179	2,178	2,217	2,521	2,573
Nebraska	1,081	1,066	1,192	1,299	1,378	1,316	1,326	1,411	1,485	1,570	1,578
Pennsylvania	5,258	6,302	7,665	8,720	9,632	9,900	10,498	11,319	11,801	11,864	11,882
Arkansas	1,128	1,312	1,574	1,752	1,854	1,949	1,910	1,786	1,923	2,286	2,351
Kentucky	1,859	2,147	2,290	2,417	2,615	2,846	2,945	3,038	3,221	3,661	3,685
New York	5,998	7,269	9,114	10,385	12,585	13,479	14,830	16,782	18,241	17,558	17,990
Oklahoma	62	1,414	1,657	2,028	2,396	2,336	2,233	2,328	2,559	3,025	3,146
Missouri	2,679	3,107	3,293	3,404	3,629	3,785	3,955	4,320	4,678	4,917	5,117
Kansas	1,426	1,470	1,691	1,769	1,871	1,801	1,905	2,179	2,249	2,364	2,478
Massachusetts	2,239	2,805	3,366	3,852	4,250	4,317	4,691	5,149	5,689	5,737	6,016
Rhode Island	346	429	543	604	687	713	792	859	950	947	1,003
Alabama	1,513	1,829	2,138	2,358	2,646	2,833	3,062	3,267	3,444	3,894	4,041
Montana	132	241	376	549	538	559	591	675	694	787	799
Illinois	3,826	4,820	5,639	6,485	7,631	7,897	8,712	10,081	11,110	11,427	11,431
Maine	661	694	742	768	797	847	914	969	994	1,125	1,228
Wisconsin	1,687	2,069	2,334	2,632	2,939	3,138	3,435	3,952	4,418	4,706	4,892
Vermont	332	344	356	352	360	359	378	390	445	511	563
Minnesota	1,302	1,748	2,076	2,387	2,564	2,792	2,982	3,414	3,806	4,076	4,375
Ohio	3,672	4,148	4,767	5,759	6,647	6,911	7,947	9,706	10,657	10,798	10,847
Indiana	2,192	2,516	2,701	2,930	3,239	3,428	3,933	4,662	5,195	5,490	5,544
Tennessee	1,747	2,015	2,180	2,338	2,616	2,916	3,292	3,566	3,926	4,591	4,877
Michigan	2,093	2,421	2,810	3,668	4,842	5,256	6,372	7,823	8,882	9,262	9,295
Louisiana	1,119	1,382	1,656	1,799	2,102	2,364	2,684	3,257	3,645	4,206	4,220
Wyoming	60	92	145	194	225	250	290	330	332	470	454
South Carolina	1,151	1,340	1,515	1,684	1,740	1,900	2,117	2,383	2,591	3,122	3,487
North Carolina	1,618	1,894	2,206	2,559	3,170	3,572	4,062	4,551	5,084	5,882	6,629
New Jersey	1,445	1,884	2,537	3,156	4,041	4,160	4,835	6,067	7,171	7,365	7,730
Idaho	78	162	326	432	445	525	589	667	713	944	1,007
Connecticut	746	908	1,115	1,381	1,607	1,709	2,007	2,535	3,032	3,108	3,287
Georgia	1,837	2,200	2,591	2,877	2,908	3,142	3,463	3,951	4,588	5,463	6,478
New Hampshire	377	412	431	443	465	492	533	607	738	921	1,109
Virginia	1,650	1,820	2,064	2,300	2,432	2,678	3,265	4,061	4,651	5,347	6,187
Delaware	168	185	202	223	238	267	318	446	548	594	666
Oregon	314	414	673	783	954	1,090	1,521	1,769	2,092	2,633	2,842
Hawaii	90	153	191	255	368	423	500	632	770	965	1,108
Maryland	1,042	1,188	1,295	1,450	1,632	1,821	2,343	3,101	3,924	4,217	4,781
Texas	2,232	3,049	3,897	4,663	5,824	6,415	7,711	9,580	11,199	14,229	16,987
Washington	349	518	1,141	1,357	1,563	1,736	2,379	2,853	3,413	4,132	4,867
New Mexico	154	195	327	360	423	532	681	951	1,017	1,303	1,515
Colorado	412	540	799	940	1,036	1,123	1,325	1,754	2,210	2,890	3,294
Utah	208	277	373	449	508	550	689	891	1,059	1,461	1,723
California	1,208	1,485	2,378	3,427	5,677	6,907	10,586	15,717	19,971	23,668	29,760
Florida	391	529	753	968	1,468	1,897	2,771	4,952	6,791	9,746	12,938
Arizona	60	120	204	334	436	499	750	1,302	1,775	2,718	3,665
Alaska	32	64	64	55	59	73	129	226	303	402	550
Nevada	46	42	82	77	91	110	160	285	489	800	1,202

Source: U.S. Bureau of the Census

TABLE 13 Population and Population Density of the 426 U.S. Coastal Counties, 1890–1990 (excluding Alaska and Hawaii)

Region	Coastal Country Land Area (sq. miles)	1890	1900	1910	1920	1930	1940	1950	1960	1970	1980	1990
		Population (in thousands)										
Gulf of Mexico	78,879	1,136	1,518	2,000	2,348	3,152	3,807	5,190	7,353	9,006	11,991	14,164
Pacific	78,502	1,277	1,636	2,920	4,040	6,328	7,448	11,241	16,172	20,485	23,835	28,760
Northeast	23,970	4,187	5,132	6,321	7,678	9,037	9,610	11,490	14,325	16,596	16,888	18,144
Southeast	37,281	689	781	904	1,083	1,373	1,732	2,433	3,992	5,257	7,159	9,289
Great Lakes	69,036	4,731	6,228	7,964	10,251	12,990	13,550	15,535	18,367	19,855	19,344	18,938
New England	27,640	6,448	8,104	10,330	11,862	14,204	15,175	16,691	18,797	20,730	20,335	21,207
Totals	315,308	18,468	23,399	30,438	37,262	47,085	51,322	62,580	79,005	91,930	99,553	110,503
		Population density per square mile										
Gulf of Mexico		14	19	25	30	40	48	66	93	114	152	180
Pacific		16	21	37	51	81	95	143	206	261	304	366
Northeast		175	214	264	320	377	401	479	598	692	705	757
Southeast		18	21	24	29	37	46	65	107	141	192	249
Great Lakes		69	90	115	148	188	196	225	266	288	280	274
New England		233	293	374	429	514	549	604	680	750	736	767
Remaining U.S.		17	20	23	26	29	31	34	38	42	48	52

Sources: U.S. Bureau of the Census and National Oceanic and Atmospheric Administration, National Ocean Service.

TABLE 14 Native and Foreign Born Population in the Coastal Counties (in thousands)

	Total Population	Native Born	Foreign Born	Pre-1950	If foreign born, arrived in U.S.			
					1950–1959	1960–1969	1970–1979	1980–1990
Gulf of Mexico	14,164	13,130	1,034	100	81	131	282	440
Pacific	28,760	22,803	5,958	304	342	695	1,621	2,996
Northeast	18,145	16,573	1,572	159	136	229	372	675
Southeast	9,289	7,896	1,392	114	87	332	282	578
Great Lakes	18,938	17,663	1,275	196	177	176	305	420
New England	21,207	17,778	3,428	399	269	546	780	1,434
Coastal Totals	110,503	95,843	14,660	1,274	1,092	2,109	3,642	6,544
Remaining U.S. (non-coastal)	138,157	133,050	5,107	569	507	684	1,228	2,120

Sources: U.S. Bureau of the Census and National Oceanic and Atmospheric Administration, National Ocean Service..

Analysis of Table 14 shows that in 1990, foreign born population accounted for 13 percent of the total in the U.S. coastal counties and just 4 percent in the non-coastal counties. Further, 60 percent of the coastal county population increase during the 1980s is due to immigrants entering the U.S. during the decade, compared to a much smaller 20 percent share in the non-coastal counties.

TABLE 15 U.S. Energy Consumption, 1960–88

	Total Energy Consumed (in trillions of BTUs)				
	1960	1970	1973	1980	1988
New England	2,049	2,881	3,157	2,669	3,064
Middle Atlantic	7,424	10,320	10,791	9,771	9,473
East North-Central	9,598	13,710	15,021	14,189	13,985
West North-Central	3,377	4,936	5,446	5,515	5,875
South Atlantic	5,000	8,304	9,712	10,555	12,318
East-South Central	2,900	4,483	5,094	5,388	5,667
West South-Central	6,816	10,987	12,991	14,610	15,103
Mountain	1,940	3,067	3,559	3,895	4,279
Pacific	4,695	7,703	8,588	9,428	10,443
Total	43,800	66,392	74,359	76,020	80,206

Source: U.S. Energy Information Administration, State Energy Data Report, Consumption Estimates, 1960–1988.

TABLE 16 World Total and Per Capita Energy Consumption Levels by Region, 1950–1986

	Total Energy Consumption (in thousand terajoules)					Per Capita Consumption (in gigajoules)				
	1950	1960	1970	1980	1986	1950	1960	1970	1980	1986
World Total	72,981	120,778	211,990	286,033	320,846	29.0	40.0	57.3	64.3	65.0
Western Europe	9,533	14,645	24,170	29,676	31,735	67.6	96.5	146.3	174.1	184.6
Southern Europe	1,507	3,429	8,038	11,364	12,348	13.8	29.0	62.6	81.9	86.5
Japan	1,571	3,296	10,538	14,039	15,060	18.8	35.0	101.0	120.2	124.1
Northern Europe	6,930	8,946	12,735	13,989	15,934	95.6	118.3	158.3	169.6	191.1
Eastern Europe	2,786	5,422	9,479	13,991	14,435	39.7	68.2	110.3	151.0	151.3
Northern America	36,760	47,710	74,397	84,873	84,465	221.3	240.2	328.5	336.9	316.4
Former U.S.S.R.	7,964	17,873	31,193	46,050	56,683	44.2	83.4	128.5	173.4	202.6
Other East Asia	58	584	1,806	3,615	4,724	1.7	14.6	34.7	57.1	68.5
China	868	8,710	9,941	18,541	24,429	1.6	13.2	12.0	18.6	22.7
Temperate South America	528	889	1,716	2,271	2,544	20.7	28.9	47.3	53.7	55.2
Oceania	774	1,286	2,397	3,460	4,163	61.2	81.5	124.0	151.8	166.8
Caribbean	226	447	1,427	1,800	1,598	13.3	21.9	57.3	61.7	50.4
Southeastern Asia	287	788	3,455	5,410	6,629	1.6	3.5	12.1	15.0	16.2
India	769	1,421	4,163	6,196	9,057	2.2	3.2	7.5	9.0	11.5
Tropical South America	668	1,640	4,925	9,384	11,111	7.8	14.1	31.8	47.3	48.8
Central America	441	899	2,158	4,238	4,878	11.8	17.8	31.0	45.7	45.5
Northern Africa	223	375	1,001	2,443	3,026	4.3	5.8	12.0	22.8	23.9
Southern Africa	681	1,100	1,792	2,788	3,290	43.3	55.3	70.1	86.1	88.3
Southern Asia (minus India)	130	387	1,743	2,883	3,425	1.0	2.5	8.7	11.1	11.1
Western Asia	178	662	1,591	4,058	6,092	4.2	11.9	21.6	41.2	51.7
Western Africa	39	97	1,150	1,841	2,211	0.6	1.2	10.9	13.0	13.0
Middle Africa	28	88	567	772	840	1.1	2.8	14.3	14.8	13.5
Eastern Africa	32	84	1,608	2,351	2,169	1.0	1.0	14.9	16.3	12.5

Sources: 1986 UN Energy Yearbook and 1990 UN Population Assessment.

Population (in thousands)						Per Capita Consumption Levels (in millions of BTUs)				
1960	1970	1973	1980	1988		1960	1970	1973	1980	1988
10,509	11,848	12,140	12,349	12,964		195	243	260	216	236
34,168	37,213	37,401	36,787	37,625		217	277	289	266	252
36,224	40,262	40,958	41,683	42,109		265	341	367	340	332
15,395	16,327	16,644	17,185	17,758		219	302	327	321	331
25,972	30,678	33,105	36,959	42,419		193	271	293	286	290
12,050	12,808	13,448	14,667	15,347		241	350	379	367	369
16,951	19,326	20,563	23,746	26,871		402	569	632	615	562
6,855	8,289	9,328	11,373	13,326		283	370	382	342	321
21,198	26,549	27,773	31,800	37,364		221	290	309	296	279
179,322	203,300	211,360	226,549	245,783		244	327	352	336	326

TABLE 17 *Economically Active Population by Region, 1950–2025*

	in agriculture (in millions)					in services and industry (in millions)			
	1950	1975	2000	2025		1950	1975	2000	2025
World Total	790.8	929.3	1,178.1	1,247.1		398.9	831.3	1,588.9	2,548.2
More Developed Regions	143.1	75.9	33.8	12.4		245.3	432.9	584.2	614.8
Less Developed Regions	647.7	853.4	1,144.3	1,234.7		153.6	398.4	1,004.7	1,933.4
Western Europe	16.4	6.6	2.4	0.3		49.2	67.0	78.6	72.0
Southern Europe	24.0	12.6	5.8	2.2		22.4	38.8	55.7	55.1
Japan	17.9	8.2	2.3	0.5		18.8	47.3	62.3	58.7
Northern Europe	4.1	2.0	1.0	0.5		29.3	35.9	42.1	41.3
Eastern Europe	17.4	11.5	5.3	2.2		18.9	35.4	48.1	52.9
Northern America	9.1	4.4	2.4	0.9		61.5	103.3	145.0	151.2
Former U.S.S.R.	52.4	28.7	12.5	4.3		41.5	98.0	140.4	167.9
Other East Asia	9.6	9.1	7.4	3.5		4.0	13.4	33.5	44.7
China	280.1	367.0	456.2	333.0		36.8	114.5	306.7	514.3
Temperate South America	2.8	2.3	1.8	1.3		7.5	12.0	18.5	25.2
Oceania	1.7	1.9	2.0	1.6		3.7	7.2	12.1	15.8
Caribbean	3.9	3.8	4.2	4.0		3.0	5.9	11.8	17.1
Southeastern Asia	66.0	84.2	106.7	98.8		18.4	48.3	129.3	245.5
India	129.8	171.9	246.1	320.0		35.6	71.3	143.3	266.1
Tropical South America	17.0	21.7	21.7	17.1		12.1	36.3	87.8	147.6
Central America	7.5	10.5	14.3	14.1		4.6	13.9	38.7	72.2
Northern Africa	11.9	13.3	17.2	16.9		4.5	12.4	36.9	83.9
Southern Africa	2.5	3.2	3.1	3.0		3.4	7.3	16.0	30.4
Southern Asia (minus India)	36.1	48.2	85.5	139.9		10.1	21.2	57.3	148.5
Western Asia	14.4	16.0	17.6	16.9		4.1	14.1	42.4	93.8
Western Africa	24.6	38.2	61.3	102.5		5.0	13.9	37.3	103.3
Middle Africa	11.4	14.8	20.2	33.1		1.5	4.6	13.9	40.9
Eastern Africa	30.1	49.2	81.0	130.7		3.0	9.4	31.2	99.8

Sources: International Labor Organization (ILO) and UN 1990 Population Assessment

TABLE 18 *Shares of U.S. Decennial Population Growth Attributable to Immigration, 1820–1990 (population in thousands)*

	Total U.S. population	Population increase in the decade	Immigrants to the U.S.	Immigrants as % share of the increase
1820	9,638			
1830	12,866	3,228	143	4
1840	17,069	4,203	599	14
1850	23,192	6,123	1,713	28
1860	31,443	8,251	2,598	31
1870	38,558	7,115	2,315	33
1880	50,189	11,631	2,812	24
1890	62,721	12,532	5,247	42
1900	76,747	14,026	3,688	26
1910	92,198	15,451	8,795	57
1920	106,005	13,807	5,736	42
1930	123,197	17,192	4,107	24
1940	132,184	8,987	528	6
1950	151,291	19,107	1,035	5
1960	179,420	28,129	2,515	9
1970	203,302	23,882	3,322	14
1980	226,546	23,244	4,493	19
1990	248,710	22,164	7,338	33

Sources: U.S. Bureau of the Census and Immigration and Naturalization Service 1990 Yearbook

This table shows that in the 1980s, legal immigration accounted for a third of population growth in the U.S. In the 1990s, and as a result of changes in immigration law, legal immigration will probably account for about half of all population growth. But even these numbers do not reflect the full impact of immigration on U.S. population. The official figures do not include illegal immigration, which contributed between 2 and 5 million additional people to the population during the 1980s. Nor does it take into account the children who are born to immigrants after they settle in this country. Calculating illegal immigration and the native-born children of all immigrants, immigration was probably the largest contributing factor to U.S. population growth in the 1980s. Without question, it will be the single greatest contributor to our growing population in the 1990s and beyond.